New Labour's Attack on Public Services

Modernisation by Marketisation? How the commissioning, choice, competition and contestability agenda threatens public services and the welfare state

Lessons for Europe

Dexter Whitfield

SPOKESMAN

This text started out as a broadsheet, became a pamphlet and then a book. Such is the scale of marketisation since Labour came to power in 1997. It has been written on trains and planes as I criss-crossed Britain and Ireland working with public bodies, trade unions and community organisations confronting the reality of marketisation and privatisation. What I hope to show is how the language and ideology of modernisation and the modernisers use marketisation to achieve endemic privatisation. I would like to thank all the organisations and people I have worked with over the last year for their invaluable input into this piece of work – in particular Kenny Bell and Newcastle City UNISON.

I thank Dorothy Calvert for her love, solidarity and support.

Dexter Whitfield

First published in 2006 by
Spokesman
Russell House, Bulwell Lane
Nottingham
NG6 0BT
Phone 0115 9708381   Fax 0115 9420433
e-mail elfeuro@compuserve.com
www.spokesmanbooks.com

© Dexter Whitfield

ISBN 0 85124 715 6
ISBN13 9780851 247151

A CIP Catalogue is available from the British Libruary.

Printed by the Russell Press Ltd., (phone 0115 9784505)

Contents

Abbreviations

ALB	Arms Length Business
ALMO	Arms length Management Organisation
BID	Business Improvement District
BSA	Building Services Association
BSF	Building Schools for the Future
CBI	Confederation of British Industry
CSR	Corporate Social Responsibility
DBFO	Design, Build, Finance and Operate
DfES	Department for Education and Skills
DH	Department of Health
DSO	Direct Service Organisation
DWP	Department for Work and Pensions
EU	European Union
FTN	Foundation Trust Network
GATS	General Agreement for Trade in Services
GP	General Practitioner
ICT	Information and Communications Technology
JVC	Joint Venture Company
LEA	Local Education Authority
LEP	Local Education Partnership
LGA	Local Government Association
LIFT	Local Improvement Finance Trust
LSP	Local Strategic Partnership
LSVT	Large Scale Voluntary Transfer
NAO	National Audit Office
NLGN	New Local Government Network
NHS	National Health Service
NOMS	National Offender Management Service
ODPM	Office of the Deputy Prime Minister
OECD	Organisation for Economic Co-operation and Development
OFSTED	Office for Standards in Education
OGC	Office of Government Commerce
OJEU	Official Journal of the European Union
PbR	Payment by Results
PCS	Public and Commercial Services Union
PCT	Primary Care Trust
PFI	Private Finance Initiative
PfH	Partnerships for Health

PfS   Partnerships for Schools
PPP   Public Private Partnership
RCE   Regional Centre of Excellence
RIA   Regulatory Impact Assessment
RSL   Registered Social Landlord
SHA   Strategic Health Authority
SSP   Strategic Service-delivery Partnership
STEPS   Strategic Transfer of the Estate to the Private Sector
TRIPs   Trade-Related Intellectual Property Rights
TUPE   Transfer of Undertakings (Protection of Employment)
          Regulations 1981
UDC   Urban Development Corporation
URC   Urban Renewal Company
VCO   Voluntary and Community Organisation
WE   Women-owned Enterprises
WTO   World Trade Organisation

Figures

1. Outsourcing of central government services in OECD countries
2. The marketisation process
3. The marketisation of education – how teachers were coralled

Tables

1. Implementation of neoliberalism by marketisation
2. Key events in marketisation and privatisation since 1980
3. Government spending by function in the European Union (2003)
4. Major areas of public sector procurement in Britain 2001-02
5. Major modernisation policy statements since 2004
6. Typology of marketisation and privatisation
7. Signed PFI projects in the UK
8. Global PPP investment by region 1990-2004
9. Winners and losers in marketisation
10. The public cost of marketisation

CHAPTER 1

What is marketisation?

Marketisation is the process by which market forces are imposed in public services, which have traditionally been planned, delivered and financed by local and central government. The process has five key elements:

● Commodifying (commercialising) services – services are changed so that they can be specified and packaged in a contract, thus extending outsourcing and offshoring.

● Commodifying (commercialising) labour – the reorganisation of work and jobs to maximise productivity and assist transfer to another employer.

● Restructuring the state for competition and market mechanisms – schools, hospitals and other facilities are compelled to compete against each other, funding is changed to follow pupils and patients, public bodies are reduced to commissioning functions creating opportunities for private finance and so-called partnerships.

● Restructuring democratic accountability and user involvement – service users are treated as consumers; services and functions are transferred to quangos; arms length companies and trusts and privately controlled companies are established within public bodies.

● Embedding business interests and promoting liberalisation internationally – business is more involved in the public policy making process and promotes national, European and global liberalisation of public services.

Most marketisation initiatives are planned, but some are outcomes of an ideological acceptance of contestability and choice. Rarely is there a 'big bang' approach. Instead, markets are created by numerous policies and initiatives in parallel with the erosion of public service principles and values and replaced with commercial values. Marketisation develops in different ways at different speeds in different services.

Markets do not evolve naturally nor do they emerge through self-regulation. States make markets – they create the conditions, regulations and financing and provide the legitimacy to create and sustain markets in public services. This is a political process as much as a technical or organisational one. Many initiatives are presented as managerial and technical in order to avoid the political responsibility and ramifications and to de-politicise the process. Different fractions of the state facilitate and promote marketisation, often made possible by the increased power of officers and managers compared with elected members.

There is broad and deep-rooted public support for public services, particularly state education and the NHS. Survey after survey demonstrates this political support and opposition to privatisation. This creates a massive problem for the marketisers – how to change user expectations and perceptions, instilling a belief that individual choice and self-interest will better meet their needs than a more collective/public interest approach, whilst cynically trying to reduce expectations of public provision but avoiding political repercussions.

State run public services in a capitalist economy have not always achieved equity of provision because of resource constraints and opposition from business and right-wing interests. There are flaws in all organisations and systems. Health, education, social care, council housing and other public services have never been isolated from markets. Although core and support services have been publicly provided, public services have had to rely on land and construction markets for new and refurbished buildings and for the supply of goods and services. There has been a series of attempts, with varying degrees of 'success', to privatise public services over the last century (Whitfield 1992 and 2001).

In plain English, marketisation is a means of establishing the dominance of commercial values, replacing central planning of social needs with market forces, and increasing private ownership and corporatisation. In particular, it extends control by transnational companies, creating new forms of accumulation and profit maximisation, and increases the exploitation of labour.

Aims and structure of this book

This book has five main objectives:
● To develop a theoretical framework to better understand the marketisation of public services.
● To identify the role of the state in creating and sustaining markets in Britain, Europe and globally.
● To examine the nature of markets in the public sector; the values, regulations, financial support and political decisions required to sustain markets.
● To make the case for the in-house provision of public services.

● To highlight alternatives and strategies that can stop, slow down and/or mitigate the negative consequences of marketisation.

The book concentrates on what is happening in Britain, which is in the vanguard of the marketisation of public services and the welfare state. The analysis is by necessity internationalist. The future of public services in Britain are directly connected with the European and World Trade Organisation (WTO) liberalisation proposals (see page 35) and the lessons from Britain should be widely used to educate and mobilise opposition across Europe and internationally.

The real danger is that if the European and World Trade Organisation liberalisation proposals are approved, they may have little effect in Britain. New Labour will have marketised to such an extent that the regulatory frameworks will already be in place.

The remainder of this chapter examines New Labour's neoliberal rationale, the wider impact of marketisation, changing values and language, and alternatives and opposition to marketisation.

Chapter 2 discusses how neoliberalism drives marketisation. It summarises the different phases of marketisation and privatisation over the last 25 years, and sets the context of the rapid growth in the services sector and the planned European Union and World Trade Organisation liberalisation of public services.

Chapter 3 discusses how markets operate in theory and in practice. It explains how markets fail, and highlights the games providers play in order to maximise profits and market share. It also describes the different types of markets, the inefficiency of markets and difficulties in making markets work in public services.

A five-stage marketisation process, consisting of the commodification of services and labour, restructuring of the state, restructuring democratic accountability and governance, and embedding business interests and promoting liberalisation internationally, is described in Chapter 4.

Chapter 5 details a typology of privatisation and marketisation of global public goods, assets and services, governance and democracy and the public domain. It provides a theoretical framework showing how the marketisation process fits into the longer-term privatisation process.

Chapter 6 is the core of the book showing how the state makes markets. It is organised around the five elements of marketisation and provides examples from across the public sector. A typology of marketisation and privatisation is presented in this chapter.

Chapter 7 details the substantial public costs incurred in marketisation and identifies the winners and losers.

The impact of marketisation on public services, sustainable development, democratic accountability, social justice, employment, and cities and regions are discussed in Chapter 8.

The last three chapters provide an alternative way forward. Chapter 9 lays out the basis of an alternative modernisation strategy, with the following chapter summarising the case for public provision. Chapter 11 discusses strategies that can be used to stop or minimise the marketisation and privatisation of public services together with examples of successful campaigns. The final chapter – Lessons for Europe – draws out the lessons to be learnt in Britain.

Reform and modernisation

'Radical reform' was widely used by the Tories in the 1980s to justify monetarist policies and the restructuring of the economy. Ironically, reform means 'a change for the better', 'to remove social and political injustices or abuses' or 'to abandon criminal habits or vices'. It can also mean 'to transform'.

In contrast, 'modernisation' is vague – 'to bring up to date' or 'to adapt to present conditions or modern ways'. Both 'reform' and 'modernisation' imply improvement and both Tory and Labour governments claim that improving the quality of public services has been their core objective. But if the application of socially useful technology, medical research and learning/knowledge are taken out of the equation, the question is whether the array of 'reform' and 'modernisation' policies over the past 25 years, and the billions spent on reorganisation and consultants, have significantly improved the quality of public services and the welfare state? Adapting the economy, labour market, public services and welfare state to the respective government's political ideology, globalisation and the demands of international capital would be a more honest rationale for their 'reform' and 'modernisation' agenda.

New Labour's neoliberal rationale

New Labour's plans are rooted in their belief that:
● Competition drives down costs.
● The private sector is more efficient than the public sector.
● Competition helps to limit producer power (by which they mean trade union power).

● Individual choice in public services will improve the quality of services.

● It is essential to provide choice for the middle class who will otherwise opt out of public services, which will be reduced to residualised services.

● Choice will reduce inequality because market forces are a more equalising mechanism than political voice, which the middle classes have traditionally used to benefit most from public services.

● Local authorities and public bodies should be restricted to commissioning in order to create the space for the private sector to develop more innovative ways of delivering services.

Contestability and choice are the new mantra of the modernisation agenda. The neo-liberal version of choice is achieved by requiring schools and hospitals to compete against each other to enable parents and patients to choose the most desirable school or hospital. Money is made to follow pupils and patients. It forces the separation between client and contractor (or purchaser/provider) and establishes a procurement and contracting process in which private and voluntary sector providers bid to take-over service delivery. Choice is also obtained by the state issuing vouchers, for example childcare vouchers, which allow users to pick and choose which service provider they will use.

Neoliberals believe that competition and user choice will force providers to improve services and invest in new facilities, driving those facilities with poorer performance, less attractive facilities and a more limited range of services to improve – the threat of going out of business and ultimate closure is deemed more effective than improving services through public management techniques.

'Contestability' is achieved by the threat of other providers entering the market thus putting pressure on the existing provider to maintain quality and efficient services. It also requires that there are no significant barriers to bar the entry or exit of other providers. So potential new entrants may force even a monopoly supplier to be efficient. In theory contestability is not the same as competition. This allows the government to claim that by promoting contestability it is not promoting outsourcing. However, this is another example of duplicitous language because in the current political context it is almost impossible to differentiate between creating the contestable conditions by which other providers challenge an existing provider and the competitive procurement regimes imposed across the public sector.

Individual marketisation policies should not be judged in isolation. They are intended to feed or leech off each other. Some policies may not work or may have unintended consequences. For example, doubts have been expressed about whether the proposals for trust schools, competition between schools and other proposals in the Education White Paper will be 'successful' (*Financial Times*, 26 October 2005). Marketisation is multi-faceted with market mechanisms in one service having a knock-on effect on competitive regimes in other services. The government is dependent on these cumulative impacts, business responding to contract and market opportunities and its ability to use regulatory frameworks to make market adjustments. Thus a community and trade union opposition, which adopts a silo mentality, treating the proposals for education, health, social care, housing, criminal justice and other services separately is doomed to have a marginal and/or temporary impact.

Labour has had relatively stable economic growth and employment since 1997 compared to the restructuring of the economy, economic crises and mass unemployment under the Tories between 1979-97. Yet New Labour has gone much further in the marketisation of public services and the welfare state than the Tories did between 1979-97. This is despite there being a high level of cooperation between the Labour Government and the trade unions – the latter have campaigned and won concessions on pensions and staff transfers, although not on the repeal of anti-trade union laws. The Warwick Agreement between Labour and the trade unions did address some policy issues, but there has been little actual or threatened industrial action over the Labour's modernisation strategy. Opposition to the Private Finance Initiative (PFI) has been channelled into technical reports, and too much of the marketisation agenda has gone unchallenged to date.

Evidence-based research is currently popular, but 'evidence' and 'research' have been in short supply in New Labour's policy-making process. Most new programmes start with pilots and pathfinders, but they are frequently mainstreamed before any evaluation is completed (for example, Local Area Agreements). New organisations are restructured no sooner than they are fully functioning, driven by financial and ideological motives devoid of any lessons from operational experience (for example, Primary Care Trusts in the NHS). Of course, there is no guarantee that if the evidence was available, that New Labour's neoliberal mindset would give it any validity. The government's approach makes a mockery of scrutiny.

What markets?

Some people believe that New Labour is not creating markets, or that it is creating 'social markets' (see below and chapter 3). But if we look at the components and structure of markets (discussed in Chapter 3) then, clearly, New Labour's modernisation is putting into place virtually all the conditions under which markets operate. It is a technicality that there is indirect rather than direct pricing in health and education – in other words, service users do not currently have to pay at the point of use. But, for example, the NHS has a price list for every treatment, and money follows patients and pupils. Service providers are driven by the price mechanism.

Education and health could not be privatised as transport or the nationalised industries were in the 1980s. Political opposition and the sheer size of any flotation or sale could destabilise financial markets. Hence, the importance of the marketisation process to create more fragmented, commodified services in a piecemeal fashion, thus allowing markets to develop, and time to wear down or buy off political opposition.

The example of the care market

It is widely accepted by government, business, health and social care professionals and the public, that there is a care market consisting primarily of residential/nursing homes and home care. Families and carers select, but the majority of costs are funded by the government. The care market was constructed by successive governments, starting with the rapid increase in the use of the residential care allowance in the 1980s, to the outsourcing (commissioning) of home care in the 1990s, both combined with closure and/or sale of local authority services. Originally described as creating a 'mixed economy' of care, the public sector now has a minor role in residential and home care provision. How markets operate is discussed more fully in Chapter 3.

The wider impact of marketisation

Marketisation is not simply about who delivers services. It has a fundamental impact on local government, democratic accountability and the welfare state. The impact on city and regional economies, the welfare state, equalities and social justice, and democratic accountability are discussed below with a wider discussion of impacts in Chapter 8.

City and regional economies
The shift from public to private/voluntary sector provision is almost
certain to have substantial impacts on local and regional economies,
particularly on the quality and level of employment and industrial
relations. Since national and international companies will dominate
larger contracts, innovation and knowledge transfer will be determined
largely by their national, European and global interests, rather than by
city and regional policies. Companies will develop production and
supply chains, which maximise the benefits for their corporate
strategies and operations. Competitive forces will drive increased
global purchasing, offshoring, and/or use of cheap migrant labour.
There is little likelihood of marketisation creating a large increase in
business and social enterprise start-ups. Marketisation of public services
means that cities have less control over their economy. Cities may be
able to 'bargain' inward investment and contract awards but only
within ever-widening public private partnership (PPP) projects.

Growth areas, particularly greenfield sites, provide a new canvas on
which marketisation can be more fully developed without the
'hindrance' of existing facilities, interests and community
accountability, in a similar way to the Bush Administration's approach
to 'restructuring' New Orleans following hurricane Katrina. A new
North-South divide could develop as marketisation develops more
rapidly in the south east/south midlands growth areas in Britain.

The expansion/reduction and new/closure of existing facilities will
increasingly be determined by market forces and the interests of the
private sector as they increase their bargaining power through
contracts and asset management/ownership. This has implications for
regional spatial strategies and the role of the state in planning,
providing and regulating markets.

The public sector accounts for 30% of employment in many
northern city economies in Britain, hence a downward spiral of job
losses and cuts in terms and conditions could have serious
consequences. A new contract economy could emerge based on
temporary and migrant contract labour resulting in a weaker and
fragmented trade union organisation.

The asset-based welfare state
The restructuring of the welfare state into an asset-based welfare state
is an integral part of the marketisation and privatisation process. The
push towards widening home ownership, child trust fund vouchers,

child-care vouchers, and the 'personalisation of pensions' are elements of the financialisation of welfare state rights and the creation of new markets. Marketisation of the welfare state is occurring through asset-based welfare products such as the Child Trust Funds (giving all new born babies £250 and encouragement to families to save via Trust funds) and Real Estate Investment Trusts ('to expand access to a wider range of savings products on a stable and well regulated basis' and to provide investment mechanisms which are an alternative to the falling value of pensions).

A new market is rapidly developing in equity release for elderly home owners to supplement low pensions and the cost of care (thus reducing family inheritance except for the wealthy). The HomeBuy shared ownership scheme is designed to extend home ownership to more council and housing association tenants.

People are being forced into individual third tier pension savings schemes as the quality of the two-pillar pension declines (Labour has continued to allow the state pension to wither on the vine – a process started by Thatcher, followed by the closure of defined benefit schemes by private companies). These initiatives help to consolidate and to expand existing markets, create new segments of markets, and create new markets for financial institutions.

Equalities and social justice
Terms such as equalities and social justice are not part of the operating system of markets. Markets do not redistribute without state intervention and regulation which, free marketeers argue, distorts the efficiency and effectiveness of markets! In place of comprehensive mandatory standards, equality policies are locally determined which has led to superficial assessment of the impact on equalities in options appraisals, procurement processes and risk assessments. Labour has focused on social inclusion of the excluded instead of social justice for all, and favours the language of the market with terms such as 'social capital' and 'stakeholders'.

There is clearly a belief that the creation of public sector markets (with the state financing and regulating markets) will afford a better degree of protection than if they were full blown commercial markets. But this is a very narrow and short-term perspective. Once markets are created it is relatively easy for this or any other government to rapidly accelerate privatisation through vouchers and similar mechanisms. It is also naïve because the private sector will constantly try to mould and change the market to increase profitability and strengthen and reinforce their control over market mechanisms. Whoever has the power, makes decisions.

The transfer of large sections of the public sector workforce to private contractors and commercialised arms-length companies is almost certain to lead to a loss of trade union membership, a weakening of trade union organisation, a watering down of demands, and more selective industrial action. Union membership is currently three times higher in the public sector than the private sector. Serving members and negotiating with a plethora of private and voluntary sector employers will consume a much higher proportion of union resources. This is likely to reduce the ability of trade unions to influence the public policy agenda, as well as the representation for equality groups.

The future of democratic accountability
Labour's modernisation policies have led to increasing centralisation of public policy making. Localism is essentially a sham. Public bodies restricted to commissioning, national procurement policies, national payment and funding systems, national/European regulatory frameworks, and contracts primarily delivered by transnational contractors and consultants expose the limitations of the localism debate.

Localism is merely the ability to tinker at the margins of centrally determined policies. For example:
● The government has established national payment systems for public money following pupils and patients and a pricing system for over 1,000 treatments.
● Central Government Department five-year plans spell out how local authorities will be required to implement choice and contestability and move from being providers of services to become mere commissioners.
● The National Procurement Strategy and the Gershon efficiency targets are national policies enforced through the Comprehensive Performance Assessment and monitored by the Regional Centres of Excellence.
● Local Area Agreements will be mandatory in all English local authorities by 2007, with all Agreements requiring negotiation with the Government Office acting on behalf of central government.
● The government continues to impose restrictions on the options that local authorities can include in options appraisal.
● Investment and funding regimes impose nationally designed and

controlled programmes such as Building Schools for the Future, which restrict locally designed responses to social needs.
● The Audit Commission, District Audit Service, Office for Standards in Education (OFSTED) and other regulatory and inspection regimes assess local authority 'progress' in addressing the centrally designed modernisation agenda which ensures that 'freedom and flexibility' as virtually meaningless.
● Reorganisation of Primary Care Trusts and Police Authorities are two examples of centrally driven projects, which further marginalise democratic accountability.

All these centrally determined policies and programmes constrain and limit what local authorities can do differently.

An increasing share of public sector contracts do not have in-house bids. This will lead to the rundown, sale of and/or closure of direct service organisations and a subsequent loss of experience in managing and providing services. The loss of capacity to deliver services will have knock-on effects such as the loss of intellectual knowledge, project management skills, and economic clout to intervene in markets, and will result in increased reliance on consultants and advisers.

Users will increasingly be caught in disputes between contractors and clients over service and financial responsibilities, interpretation of contract clauses, and legal disputes.

Corporatisation and the corporate welfare complex
The increasing power of transnational corporations lies not just in the production and sale of goods and services but also in branding and defining values through the media and information and communications technology, the concentration of ownership of land and resources, the funding of research and political organisations, and in the global, regional, national and local institutional policy making process.

There are two parallel processes in operation. Firstly, there is the erosion of direct democratic accountability as responsibilities are transferred from public services to arms length companies. Community participation or 'citizen engagement' is used as a smoke screen to conceal less accountability and transparency.

Secondly, there is the increased power of private companies and business interests in the public policy making process and the delivery of public services. The attempt to impose 'corporate citizen' and corporate social responsibility on public sector organisations such as the NHS, for example, is symptomatic of reducing standards, de-politicisation, and a power shift to business as a result of the emergence of a corporate welfare complex (Whitfield, 2001). The NHS is a public body with responsibility for health care and the public health of the nation state. To claim that it should be treated as a private company, and to the same business standards, is nonsensical. This would deny the public functions, duties and responsibilities of the state, government and public bodies. It is in effect dragging the state and public sector down to private sector standards, instead of the reverse.

A corporate welfare complex is emerging that consists of contractors, transnational corporations, financial institutions, consultants, business associations and politicians. It has four main parts:

● A contract services system with a shared client/contractor ideology, contract culture, value system and vested interests;
● An owner-operator infrastructure industry consisting of the major financial institutions, construction companies, facilities management companies, and private finance initiative advisers from a continual stream of design, build, finance and operate (DBFO) projects, and the acquisition of project via refinancing on the secondary market.
● A system of regulatory and financial concessions to business such as tax relief, public subsidies, local and regional grants.
● The corporatisation of public bodies and business involvement in public policy making (Whitfield, 2001 and 2002, Farnsworth, 2004).

Marketisation feeds the growth and power of this complex.

The third sector alternative

New opportunities for social enterprises? In addition to supporting small and medium-sized enterprises (SMEs), procurement and marketisation is supposed to provide new opportunities for voluntary and community organisations (VCOs), black minority-owned enterprises (BMEs), women-owned enterprises (WEs), and social enterprises generally. However, outsourcing services and functions to these organisations is no different in principle from outsourcing to a private contractor. The only exception would be when a new or existing social enterprise was supported, when an in-house option was not possible. Certainly most of the larger multi-service contracts are out of reach of social enterprises and community organisations. Furthermore, the track record of many voluntary organisations is questionable, and the sector is not noted for democratic accountability.

The housing association sector has changed radically in the last 30 years, since the 1974-79 Labour Government expanded their role and redirected public spending from local authorities on spurious grounds of efficiency. The sector is dominated by national and regional housing associations, many having diversified into social care and regeneration partnerships with private developers.

Lessons should be drawn from Australia where Federal and State governments have developed contractual and quasi-contractual relationships with the voluntary sector for some time. Larger voluntary organisations have tended to capture the bulk of contracts, although they represent a minority of voluntary organisations. This is resulting in 'an increasing polarisation within the sector between the majority consisting of smaller, voluntaristic and less sophisticated organisations, and the minority of wealthy, professionalised, corporate, employing organisations' (Butcher, 2005). Butcher refers to a study which concluded that 'as voluntary organisations grow and come to rely on paid employees to fulfil their mission, they substitute finance capital for social capital. Their reduced reliance on social capital leads them, in turn, to reproduce less of it' (ibid).

It often suits governments to 'laud the contributions' of voluntary organisations, which can exaggerate the ability and value of the voluntary sector. Butcher, drawing on McDonald, concludes that these attributes often contain 'elements of myth' which, in turn, 'are used to legitimate the sector's role and "reinforce the notion that a mixed economy of service delivery is reliant on it"' (ibid).

Changing values and language

But many markets are inefficient and fail. Governments are forced to impose rules and regulations to protect the public and service users from market abuse, exploitative prices, private monopoly and corporate greed.

So the marketeers and privatisers have a problem. They resort to denials, half-truths and lies. Some go to inordinate lengths to try to set out a case as to how their 'reforms' or 'modernisation' will produce benefits for all, and that they are not creating markets nor privatising services. A whole new body of words and phrases has been developed to mask and conceal true intentions and impose new business values.

They are even resorting to invoking memories of the cooperative movement and mutualism in a desperate attempt to sell their policies.

Best Value was heralded in 1998 by the four 'C's of challenge, compare, consult and competition as the four elements of service reviews. The first three have been marginalised as modernisation has been widened by the choice and personalisation agenda, and have been replaced by:

● Care brokers and job brokers
● Charging
● Choice
● Clients
● Coasting
● Commissioning
● Community Interest Companies
● Competition
● Contestability
● Contracts
● Corporate citizen or responsibility
● Independent sector
● Local partners
● Personalisation
● The 'offer'

But there is one 'c' word which is missing – class.

The Office of the Deputy Prime Minister five-year plan constantly makes reference to 'our offer'. This is the language of the marketplace. It also suggests a denial of responsibility of the state by implying a 'take it or leave it' attitude to local government with no room for negotiation or flexibility.

The so-called 'independent' sector is dominated by private companies. The mask of 'independent' sector status is often used as a means of trying to neutralise politically the transfer of services to the private sector. Similarly, the encouragement of social enterprises and 'community providers' in criminal justice, education, and other services serves the same function.

The globalisation debate and the World Trade Organisation trade liberalisation negotiations are also shrouded in acronyms, jargon and often unintelligible language.

Lack of ideological and intellectual rigour
Some modernisers claim that outsourcing and partnerships are not

marketisation and privatisation. There has been a stream of denials and disingenuous statements by ministers and senior public sector managers. The Secretary of State for Health, Patricia Hewitt's annual health and social care lecture at the London School of Economics is such an example.

> '*We are often accused of introducing a "market" in to the NHS. But although I have described, very fully and I am afraid at some length, the changes we are making, I have not once used the word "market".*'
>
> *I do not believe that we are turning the NHS into a market, and nor do I think that we should ...Yes, we are giving patients and users more choice. Yes, we are giving providers more freedom to innovate and, where it is appropriate, to compete against each other. And where we mean 'competition', we should say so, instead of pretending that 'contestability' is something different. Yes, money will follow the patient ... Why should the use of the private sector, when it gives us new hospitals, when it benefits patients and the public, have to mean 'privatisation'?*
>
> *What we are creating – not only in health and social care, but in education and many other public goods – are not markets, but modern public services* (Hewitt, 2005).

Harold Pinter referred to 'political language' in his Nobel acceptance speech. Politicians 'are interested not in truth but in power and in the maintenance of that power. To maintain that power it is essential that people remain in ignorance, they live in ignorance of the truth, even the truth of their own lives. What surrounds us therefore is a vast tapestry of lies, upon which we feed' (Pinter, 2005).

Statements such as the 'NHS free at the point of use' are meaningless because the health service could be entirely provided by the private sector and remain funded by the state with the basic service free at the point of use. But once the private sector had a powerful role in service delivery it would ensure that 'free at the point of use' would have less and less meaning or truth.

Advocates of contestability, competition, markets, public-private partnerships and outsourcing often claim that 'it is not privatisation', but this is a denial of theory and practice. Privatisation is not limited to the transfer of physical assets from the public to the private sector. It is 'playing with words' to argue otherwise. The motive behind this approach is essentially to play down the scope and scale of planned privatisation to elected members, staff and the public. In other circumstances this is usually called deception.

Strategic partnerships have been claimed not to be privatisation when it is patently obvious that work previously carried out by the public sector is outsourced to private firms, often with long-term contracts. Staff are transferred to a private or voluntary sector employer (in some cases seconded and managed by a private contractor), and other assets such as equipment and intellectual property are transferred to a private contractor.

Outsourcing 'enables the immigration staff to fulfil their primary role' claimed the Home Office recently in response to PCS criticism that a clause in the Asylum and Nationality Bill could lead to outsourcing of freight and vehicle searches (*Financial Times*, 27 October 2005).

Alternatives and opposition

There is an alternative to the marketisation and privatisation version of modernisation. This is discussed in Chapter 9.

There is deep-seated and significant opposition to government policies, particularly in health and education. Many officers and elected members are delaying and slowing down the implementation of government policies, often 'going through the motions' to keep inspectors from producing critical reports on the performance of their authorities. The government has created a climate in which many officers and elected members do not have confidence to speak out for fear of jeopardising career paths and political ambitions. They are very unhappy with the direction of change but are afraid to speak out because Labour has constructed a scenario where a marketised version of modernisation is 'the only show in town'.

There are clear signs of growing opposition to New Labour's modernisation by marketisation strategy. The campaign for a fourth option for council housing, largely run by Defend Council Housing, is a good example of combining local and national action, Parliamentary lobbying, and policy analysis with organising and support for tenants campaigns. The Keep Our NHS Public campaign is another clear indication that health service workers, trade unions and community organisations are committed to combat the marketisation of the health service. A series of strategies are discussed in Chapter 11.

CHAPTER 2

Neoliberalism drives marketisation

The neoliberal context and its drivers

Neoliberalism is a conservative economic philosophy which revived in the late 1970s following the crisis in Keynesian economics, escalating inflation at the end of the post-war reconstruction boom, the soaring cost of the US war in Vietnam and the 1973 oil shock. Governments had difficulty financing budget deficits, which led to the imposition of restrictive monetary policies and cuts in public expenditure. The Thatcher and Reagan government's in the 1980s abandoned the policy of state intervention to maintain full employment. They deregulated financial and labour markets, reduced corporate and top personal tax rates, privatised public assets, promoted free trade and small government.

Developing countries were subjected to similar policies as aid from the World Bank, the International Monetary Fund (IMF) and other international agencies was conditional on similar deregulation and privatisation policies, achieving macroeconomic stability mainly by cutting public spending and subsidies to the poor and opening economies to foreign trade and finance.

Neoliberalism has eight key components:

Liberalisation and competition – free trade and competition to determine who delivers services. Acceptance of globalisation as a benign force and facilitating the internationalisation of free inward and outward flows of money, goods, services and labour.

Markets – a belief in superiority of markets in allocating resources and organising the economy.

Deregulation of financial markets – permitting the free flow of capital globally and new opportunities for accumulation.

Reconfiguring the role of the state – abandoning demand management, reduced intervention, restructuring and reorganising service delivery by limiting the role of government to commissioning, coupled with withdrawal of public provision. National economic and spatial strategy based primarily on the needs of capital. A narrow performance management approach to public management.

Privatisation – of public assets and services, governance and democracy and the public domain (see Chapter 6).

Consumerism – restructuring public services and the welfare state towards consumerism, individualism and personalisation, shopping for services and the pursuit of self-interest, and the erosion of public, collective and community interest.

Labour market flexibility and deregulation – abandoning interventionist strategies to maintain full employment, expansion of casual and migrant labour, limiting trade union organisation and activity, and reinforcing management's 'right to manage'.

Increasing the power of business coupled with the erosion of democratic accountability and transparency – partnerships, decentralisation of functions but centralisation of policy, depoliticisation of civil society and voluntary organisations drawn into service delivery, citizens treated merely as consumers despite neoliberal rhetoric of participation and empowerment.

How marketisation embeds neoliberalism

The marketisation of public services plays a key role in embedding neoliberalism in the economy. This is demonstrated in Table 1 (see page 25) which shows how marketisation contributes to and supports each component part of neoliberalism. Readers are also referred to the typology of privatisation and marketisation in Chapter 5.

Marketisation drives the privatisation agenda

Once services are marketised or partially privatised, a process begins which generates escalating levels of marketisation and privatisation.

Arms length companies seek further independence: Once arms length companies and trusts are established, they seek to move further away from the public sector. This is driven by a number of factors including the vested interests of senior management wishing to protect their higher pay levels, and the formation of national trade groups to represent the 'interests' of arms length bodies. They also demand additional 'freedoms and flexibilities'.

Markets spawn brokers or middle agents: The use of direct payment systems and individual budgets in the social care and employment services has already triggered the 'need' for care brokers and job brokers respectively. School brokerages have been created to act as a middle agent between a school and an array of private contractors seeking to provide schools with goods and services (for example, in Essex and Rotherham). This function was previously carried out by the Local Education Authority or via public sector purchasing bodies. The use of brokers and agents diverts work away from public

Table 1: *Implementation of neoliberalism by marketisation*

Components of Neoliberalism	How marketisation embeds neoliberalism
Liberalisation and competition	Liberalisation of public services at national, European and global levels creating vast new markets and new forms of accumulation. Outsourcing to private and voluntary sectors. Schools and hospitals become stand-alone businesses and compete for pupils and patients. Transnational companies win increasing proportion of public service contracts and create new PFI/PPP consortia. Increased offshoring of work. International takeovers and mergers of private contractors.
Markets	Choice of provider, competition between providers and financial restructuring to allow public money to follow service users creates markets. Privately financed infrastructure creates new markets. Growth of secondary financial markets to refinance PFI projects and consortia selling equity stakes plus growth of market intermediaries such as agents and brokers in social care, education and employment services. Public bodies required to create markets and involve business in the packaging of contracts.
Deregulation of financial markets	Foreign financial institutions help to finance stock transfers and PFI/PPPs and also encourages British investment, including pension funds, in PPPs and privatisation overseas.
Reconfiguring role of the state	Commissioning and procurement dominate public management which includes options appraisals, in-house bids, managed reduction, closures, and decline of public provision. Performance management regimes of targets, benchmarking and inspections with reward and punishment. The Private Finance Initiative and new models such as NHS Local Improvement Finance Trust and Building Schools for the Future, together with Strategic Service-delivery Partnerships (SSPs) are reconfiguring the financial and operational relationship with private capital being more fully embedded within the public domain and national infrastructure. Neoliberal claim of 'government failure' in response to concept of market failure (because of asymmetry of information, lack of trust, poor contractor performance, poor regulatory frameworks).

Components of Neoliberalism	How marketisation embeds neoliberalism
Privatisation	Erosion of welfare state, use of vouchers, direct payments and individual budgets. Minimal redistribution. Erosion of public service ethos and values, replaced by business values and individual responsibility. Conceal public impact and cost of policies. Greater responsibility on the family and individuals for the reproduction of labour and the costs of education and caring.
Consumerism	Propaganda campaign to promote choice agenda and patient/pupil/user-led services despite surveys which show that people want good quality local services. Fewer than one in five people think of themselves as consumers or customers and more than half of staff and those using services regard the relationship as being members of the local community or wider public (Economic and Social Research Council, 2006).
Labour market flexibility and deregulation	The commodification (commercialisation) of labour. Transfer of staff from public to private sector, wider use of casual and migrant labour. Widening levels of subcontracting further fragment provision. Demands for increased productivity/efficiency and increased flexibility of labour. Devolved organisations such as arms length companies and trusts strengthen management's 'right to manage' and ability to localise terms and conditions. Attempt to weaken trade union organisation and representation and erode historical gains.
Increasing the power of business coupled with erosion of democratic accountability and transparency	Reconfiguring the public domain – changing the governance and accountability of public institutions. Centralisation of public policy making but masked by claims of localism and decentralisation. Functions transferred to private sector or to less accountable quangos, arms length companies and trusts. Partnerships on every menu. Erosion of democratic accountability, less transparency and emergence of corporate welfare complex as transnational companies gain market share and bigger role in public policy making process.

providers and creates sub-markets which are often outside regulatory frameworks.

Primary care trusts in Greater Manchester have created a centralised Commissioning and Contract Business Services which will provide specifications, procurement, negotiate on price, volume and quality, and monitor contracts for Trusts and GP practices under practice-based commissioning (*Health Service Journal*, 1 December 2005). Third party agents such the Evercare programme operated by UnitedHealth Europe (UnitedHealth Group, USA) provide case management services for frail, elderly patients. The Department of Health invited Evercare to run nine pilot sites in Britain. For example, three primary care trusts in Bristol and South Gloucestershire recruited ten advanced practice nurses for the project, partially funded by the Department of Health (Bristol North Primary Care Trust, 2003). Few could disagree with the principles of these types of services, but they should be part of the core public service, rather than a privatised agency service.

The Education White Paper promises a network of 'choice advisers' who will 'offer independent, unbiased advice and raise the interest, expectations and aspirations of those who may not previously have felt they had any real choice' (DfES, 2005). The government will provide £12m funding over the next two years.

The Housing Corporation recently appointed 23 housing associations to be 'zone agents' to promote and administer the new HomeBuy low cost home ownership scheme. The 'zone agents' cover 37 zones in England and will market the three HomeBuy schemes (see page 99) and direct eligible applicants to local schemes.

Takeovers and mergers: Freed from direct democratic accountability and corporate responsibilities, many senior managers become entrepreneurial and want to 'build businesses' by taking over or merging with similar organisations in neighbouring authorities.

Diversification into other services: The pressure to diversify intensifies because of the loss of economies of scale – new stand-alone arms length companies lose the benefits of being part of larger organisations – and because of financial pressures. They are likely to commence bidding for related public services.

User charges: A pricing culture develops in which services are further commodified so that charges can be introduced, for example by dividing the service into different components to create the illusion of choice and ability to charge for a wider range of 'additional' services.

Competition intensifies: Competition intensifies between different schools, hospitals, and other services – as stand alone businesses they must 'compete' to survive. This will lead to 'success or failure' spurring further takeovers and mergers as market forces and competitive regimes erode public service values and principles.

Housing leads the way

Council housing and the role of local government in the provision of homes have been marketised for a considerable time. 'What happens to housing today happens to other public services tomorrow' has been a truism for too long. Council housing has witnessed the largest asset sale (over one million homes sold to tenants), the largest subsidised privatisation (£millions in discounts), the largest transfer of assets to third sector organisations (one million homes transferred to housing associations to date), and had one of the largest diversions of responsibilities and resources from local government to the third sector as housing associations took over housing improvement work after 1974. The third sector was deemed more efficient and innovative although not a scrap of evidence was ever produced to support this assertion.

Whilst the housing sector is structurally different from other public services, the history of council housing demonstrates clearly the extent to which the state and business will go to marketise and privatise. If you think state education and the NHS are 'safe in their hands', then think again.

Phases of marketisation and privatisation

There have been three distinct phases of marketisation and privatisation since the early 1980s.

The first phase of neoliberalism in Britain began in the 1980s, focused on 'rolling back' state interference in the economy and promoting free market ideology, deregulating labour markets and fracturing trade union power. This period saw the large-scale sale of nationalised industries, utilities and state owned industrial corporations, in addition to the right to buy for council tenants. There was significant restructuring for privatisation but the period saw sell-offs rather than any rolling back of the state in the economy.

The second phase began in the early 1990s with increased emphasis on competition, commercialisation and quasi markets in public services. Competitive tendering was extended in central and local government to white-collar services, with markets imposed in core services such as health and education, which could not be privatised for political and economic reasons in the same way as nationalised industries had been. The establishment of Agencies led to the growth of performance management, later extended by Labour's Best Value regime, which removed compulsory competition in local government but extended competition to all services via options appraisals. The commissioning concept, requiring the separation of client and contractor responsibilities, with the state being responsible only for client functions, was mainstreamed in social care and later housing with varying degrees of 'success'. This phase also saw the emergence of public service consumerism and consultation. Most significantly, private investment in public services commenced. By the end of the 1990s transport, energy, utilities, telecommunications and industrial state owned corporations had been privatised leaving the social infrastructure of the welfare state (education, health, council housing, leisure), defence, security, and the criminal justice system still in public ownership.

The third phase of neoliberalism began in the early 2000s with a new emphasis on making markets in most public services. Commissioning and contestability became paramount with the government sanctioning the use of public sector assets and intellectual capital to fulfil these objectives. Again, the state was not 'rolled back' or 'hollowed out' but reconfigured and transformed into making, supporting and sustaining markets. There was also a rapid increase in arms length public/private organisations such as foundation hospitals and foundation schools, arms length management organisations, urban development corporations, urban regeneration companies, outsourcing to strategic partnerships and local public service boards. Privately dominated local educational partnerships and other public private partnership models were imposed within the public sector.

Further phases of neoliberalism could develop with the provision of core services (teaching, medical services) by the private sector, outsourcing of management, new Building Schools for the Future and Local Improvement Finance Trust-type models, and development of vouchers and similar direct payment systems.

Within the three phases of neoliberalism there have many key events in the marketisation and privatisation over the last 25 years (see Table 2). There have been phases of competitive tendering at the beginning of each decade, commencing with manual workers in the early 1980s, extending to white collar services in the 1990s, and encompassing all services after 2000. Labour's abolition of Compulsory Competitive Tendering has been completely reversed with the mainstreaming of contestability and competition. The transfer/sale of services/assets to arms length companies, private companies, and third sector organisations in the 1990s has continued after a brief lull.

Table 2: *Key events in marketisation and privatisation since 1980*

Date	Key events in marketisation and privatisation
Conservative Government 1979-1997	
1980s	Disposal of public land and buildings including sale of council housing. Efficiency campaign launched. Compulsory tendering of defined manual services in local government from 1980, widened in 1988, and management directive to tender NHS support services from 1983.
1981-96	Privatisation of nationalised industries, state corporations, transport, utilities, telecoms, and land and property with gross proceeds of £123 billion.
1991-97	Internal market in health – public funding switched from geographical distribution to individual hospitals, which became Trusts. Separation of client and contractor roles.
1992	Private capital investment for infrastructure projects commenced with the Private Finance Initiative (PFI).
1990s	Compulsory tendering extended to local government white collar services. Internal markets focus in public management reform. Commissioning of community care leads to widespread outsourcing. Competing for Quality tendering in civil service. Transfer/sale of services/assets to 327 arms length companies, private companies and third sector organisations.
New Labour Government 1997	
1998	Compulsory tendering terminated in local government but competition embedded in Best Value service review regime and applicable to all services. Increasing emphasis on performance management through targets and inspection regimes.

Date	Key events in marketisation and privatisation
2000	Marketisation and procurement take centre stage in government modernisation agenda. World Trade Organisation starts new round of negotiations for General Agreement for Trade in Services (GATS). Decent Homes Standard launched with options appraisal limited to stock transfer, private finance initiative, and arms length management company.
2001	NHS Local Improvement Finance Trust (LIFT) launched for improving inner city health centres and surgeries. First Strategic Service-delivery Partnerships (SSPs) commenced in Lincolnshire, Middlesbrough, Bedfordshire and Liverpool.
2003	National Procurement Strategy launched for local government.
2004	European Union publishes draft Directive on Internal Services Market. New efficiency campaign for £21.5bn public expenditure savings launched with 2004 Spending Review. Building Schools for the Future (BSF) programme launched using Local Education Partnerships with 80% private sector control and academies. Regional Centres of Excellence established for procurement and efficiency. National Offender Management System (NOMS) launched with contestability and competition for probation and prison services.
2005	Choice, personalisation, foundation model and new localism promoted in departmental five-year plans. Independence, Well-being and Choice Green Paper on Adult Social Care. Education White Paper proposing trust schools, academies, local education authorities reduced to commissioning organisations. Restructuring of Primary Care Trusts. National procurement strategy for Fire and Rescue Service. World Trade Organisation GATS negotiations in Hong Kong make marginal 'progress'.
2006	A new Deal for Welfare: Empowering People into Work – White Paper from Department of Work and Pensions. Our Health, Our Care Our Say: A New Direction for Community Services, White Paper from Department of Health.

Source: Whitfield 1992, 2001 and updated.

Globalisation and growth of services

The growth of the services sector

Services accounted for 70% of gross domestic product in most Organisation for Economic Co-operation and Development countries in 2002, a marked increase since the 1970s. Services account for about 75% of employment in Britain, Canada and the United States compared to much lower shares, below 60%, in several European countries. Telecommunications, transport, wholesale and retail trade, finance, insurance and business services accounted for 60% of all new jobs created in the OECD area in the past decade.

'Several important services, such as health, education and social services, are often provided in a non-market environment, although with considerable variation across countries. The absence of a price mechanism implies that it is difficult for the – often non-profit – providers of these services to gauge demand, which is sometimes reinforced by the absence of competition between providers and reliance on public funding. As a result of this environment, producers may have difficulties in responding adequately to evolving users' needs, such as the growing demand for long-term health care. Suitable policy measures, which could be explored in several public services, include the opening up of markets to private providers, the introduction of user choice, linking public funding more closely to performance as well as user payments. While such measures may not be suitable for all public services, for example, because they conflict with fundamental equity objectives, such policy changes may contribute to better and more targeted services in several areas, and may help enhance efficiency while also achieving key public policy objectives' (Growth in Services, OECD, 2005). This statement demonstrates how far neoliberalism is embedded in the OECD. Remember this when you read their Country Reports!

New markets and sources of accumulation

In crude terms, business interests perceive the public sector as a multi-billion market. The British government already spends £120 billion per annum purchasing goods and services from the private sector (a small proportion from the voluntary sector). Business and right wing political interests have never been happy that the public sector delivers many of its own services and has consistently sought to challenge and undermine public service provision. For business it represents a vast new market. The business case to marketise and privatise public services to provide access to this vast new market is couched in terms of efficiency and value for money, but they are just part of a self-fulfilling propaganda war.

Market forecasts

Public sector outsourcing in Britain is forecast to increase from the current figure of £45bn to over £67bn by the end of 2006/07 (Kable,

Table 3: *Government spending by function in the European Union (2003) (billion Euro)*

	Education	Health	Housing & community amenities	Recreation culture & religion	Economic affairs	Social protection	Total general Government expenditure
Austria	13.1	14.9	1.6	2.2	11.7	48.4	114.9
Belgium	17.0	18.9	0.8	3.3	13.2	48.8	137.5
Cyprus	0.7	0.4	0.5	0.1	0.7	1.3	5.3
Czech'	3.9	5.2	0.7	1.0	9.3	11.7	42.6
Denmark	15.9	10.8	10.8	3.1	6.9	47.2	105.6
Estonia	0.5	0.3	0.1	0.2	0.3	0.8	2.9
Finland	9.5	9.3	0.6	1.8	7.2	31.0	73.1
France	95.1	132.5	14.1	12.6	75.7	333.7	849.5
Germany	88.0	138.5	24.7	14.7	83.7	485.0	1,041.3
Greece	5.5	4.4	0.7	0.7	8.6	32.0	73.8
Hungary	4.4	4.1	0.8	1.6	4.1	12.4	36.5
Ireland	6.1	9.4	2.7	0.7	6.4	13.6	46.4
Italy	68.0	84.5	10.6	11.8	49.4	238.7	637.2
Latvia	0.6	0.3	0.1	0.1	0.4	1.1	3.5
Lithuania	1.0	0.7	0.1	0.1	0.7	1.6	5.6
Lux'bourg	1.3	1.3	0.2	0.5	1.2	4.6	10.9
Malta	0.3	0.3	0.1	0.0	0.4	0.6	2.1
Neth'land	23.5	21.5	7.6	5.1	25.6	84.4	222.5
Poland	11.6	5.6	2.7	1.5	5.9	36.8	82.4
Portugal	9.1	9.3	1.1	1.6	5.7	20.5	62.2
Slovakia	1.3	0.7	0.3	0.3	1.5	4.5	11.3
Slovenia	1.4	1.7	0.1	0.2	0.9	4.5	11.8
Spain	32.9	32.9	8.2	10.2	33.0	100.5	294.9
Sweden	19.8	19.5	2.4	2.9	13.3	66.6	156.8
UK	85.1	107.8	11.6	10.1	52.3	261.8	692.8
Total EU	**515.6**	**642.8**	**93.9**	**86.7**	**418.2**	**1,892.3**	**4,723.4**

Source: General Government Expenditure by Function in the EU in 2003, Eurostat, August 2005.

2004). Local government's share is currently about £6bn, which is expected to increase by about 16% over the next four years.

European Union public spending on services

Government expenditure by the twenty-five countries in the European Union in 2003 included 643 billion Euros on health and 515 billion Euros on education (see Table 3). Economic affairs accounted for 418 billion Euros with other services such as housing and community amenities and recreation, culture and regions accounting for much smaller levels of expenditure. Defence, public protection and environmental protection expenditure was 170, 166 and 72 billion Euros respectively.

Table 3 also highlights the very large potential markets available in Germany, France, Italy, Spain, Netherlands and Britain, and the very wide differential in the level of government spending within the European Union.

The size of potential markets is indicated by the percentage of public expenditure as a percentage of total expenditure on health and education (although this does not take account of the existing level of outsourcing). In the 29 OECD countries the health expenditure accounts for 83.4% of total expenditure on health in the UK, which is bettered by six countries (OECD, 2005). Public expenditure accounts for between 65% – 80% of total health expenditure in most countries, the exceptions being the United States, Mexico and Korea with under 50%, and Greece with public expenditure accounting for just over half total health expenditure.

Public expenditure in education accounted for a higher percentage of total expenditure with a country mean of 88%. The UK figure was below the mean at 85%. Korea and the US had the lowest percentages at 58% and 69% respectively.

Public procurement
Britain leads OECD countries in the outsourcing of government services (see Figure 1). The level on Britain is significantly higher than the United States and other major European economies such as Germany, and more than twice the level in France and Italy.

Figure 1: *Outsourcing of Central Government Services in OECD countries*
Relative Index 0=Lowest; 1=Highest

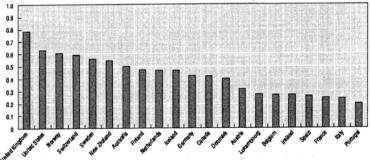

Source: Public Sector Modernisation: The Way Forward, OECD, 2005.

Public sector procurement is highly variable between services, illustrated in Table 4. Of the UK expenditure of £3bn on highways in 2001/02 the public sector accounted for 98% of the expenditure in contrast to professional services where the public sector accounted for just 12.8% in the same period. The level of expenditure on construction and information technology were considerably higher.

Table 4: *Major areas of public sector procurement in Britain 2001-02*

Sector	UK Expenditure (£bn)	Total public sector expenditure (£bn)	% public sector
IT*	22.6	12.4	55.0
Highways	3.0	3.0	98.0
Construction	81.8	25.4	31.1
Professional services	4.7	0.6	12.8

Source: Increasing Competition and Improving Long-Term Capacity Planning in the Government Market Place, OGC, 2003
* 2003/04 projections.

European and global liberalisation of public services

The liberalisation of public services is being planned by both the European Union through a new Directive on the Internal Market for Services and by the World Trade Organisation through the General Agreement on Trade in Services.

European Union Internal Market for Services
A draft Services Directive was published in January 2004 but its progress was slowed following the 'no' votes on the European Constitution in France and the Netherlands, which were in part due to opposition to the draft Services Directive and the affirmation of neoliberalism in the EU constitution. The European Parliament is expected to vote on the Directive in 2006. Each EU member will then have to introduce regulations to implement the Directive, which will come into force in 2010.

The European Commission wants to liberalise the cross border supply of services to create a single market across the 25 European countries. It wants to eliminate all barriers which may make it more difficult, costly, or less profitable for a service provider to operate in one country compared to another. This includes removing restrictions, deregulation and reducing red tape.

The European Union (and the World Bank) do not use the term 'public services'. Instead the European Union refers to 'Services of General Interest' which include collective and universal services such as education, public administration, pensions, criminal justice system, telecommunications and utilities. The Treaty of Amsterdam in 1999 emphasized that 'Services of General Economic Interest' include services which have a cross-border function such as transport, energy, water, communications (generally services for which users make payments), but also include health and social services.

The aim of the draft Services Directive is to encourage cross border trade, give service providers the freedom to establish their business in any member state, and to facilitate the free movement of services between member states. The European Union claims that the Directive will improve economic growth and employment.

The draft Services Directive will apply to 'any economic activity normally provided for remuneration' regardless of the purpose of the activity and who pays for it. The Directive is designed to cover business services (facilities management, management consultancy), services provided both to businesses and consumers (construction, legal and financial advice, security services) and consumer services (such as health care services, sport and leisure services). Charlie McCreevy, European Commissioner for Internal Market and Services, made commitments to exclude 'health and publicly funded services of general interest' (McCreevy, 2005).

The Directive will also apply to activities that are already open to competition and, to this extent, will not require member states to privatise public services or to abolish existing monopolies. However, most public services in Britain are already open to various degrees of competition and could therefore be within the scope of the Directive.

The impact of the Directive will almost certainly mean that more services are subjected to competition and procurement. More intense competition is likely in some services as a result of cross-border bidding. Some contractors will inevitably try to exploit loopholes by using agents, subcontractors and migrant labour. There are likely to be numerous legal disputes about whether services are within the scope of the Directive.

The European Parliament voted overwhelming for a compromise draft Directive in February 2006 which excluded the country of origin proposals, services of general interest and some services of general economic interest, such as healthcare, and labour laws. The position on education and whether all social services are excluded remains unclear. A modified Directive will be drawn up by the Commission.

Meanwhile, the European Commission is making a big push to require developing countries to liberalise trade in services, masked by the European Union's commitment to development and poor countries. 'We want to liberalise trade and grow markets in which to sell European goods and services,' stated Trade Commissioner Peter Mandelson (Curtis, 2005). The European Union is making development assistance conditional on liberalising services and adopting an aggressive stance in demanding poor countries benchmark liberalisation of key sectors. They are also demanding commitments to liberalise government procurement, well beyond the requirements of the World Trade Organisation Government Procurement regulations, which focus on transparency, not liberalisation (ibid).

WTO General Agreement for Trade in Services
The World Trade Organisation is continuing to negotiate the General Agreement on Trade in Services (GATS), which is, essentially, modelling the same marketisation principles to create a global market in services. The European Union and the British government are supporting the WTO proposals.

The scope of the GATS is very broad. Services provided 'in the exercise of government authority' are claimed to be exempt, but these are narrowly defined as services provided neither on a commercial basis nor a competitive basis (GATS article 1:3.c). 'Accordingly, if a service is provided exclusively by government on a not-for profit basis then the exclusion likely applies, but having *either* commercial *or* competitive elements present in the financing or delivery of a service would negate the protective effect of the governmental authority exclusion. Because most so-called 'public service' systems, including those at the local government level, are actually mixed public-private systems with varying degrees of private financing and delivery of services, the governmental authority exclusion cannot be relied upon for protection from GATS rules (Sinclair, 2005).

Trade in services under GATS has four dimensions or modes:

Mode One: *Cross Border Supply* – the provision of public services from one country to another.

Mode Two: *Consumption Abroad* – this is where consumers or their property travel to another country to obtain a service. For example,

UK nationals travelling abroad to have an operation paid for by the NHS.

Mode Three: *Commercial Presence* – this is where a service provider (public or private) would set up in another country and covers all foreign investment.

Mode Four: *Presence of Natural Persons* – covers persons travelling to deliver services in other countries.

The UK government has constantly maintained its commitment to trade liberalisation and consistently contended that public services will not fall within the remit of the regulations (DTI, 2002). However, it is increasingly difficult to identify the boundaries of public services, particularly where public goods are privately financed and/or delivered through competitive procurement.

Employment impact of services market liberalisation

The estimates of the global benefits of trade liberalisation have fallen dramatically over the past two years – they are now a third of previous levels, whilst the benefits to developing countries are now a fifth of previous levels. A review of the Global Trade Analysis Project (GTAP) and the World Bank LINKAGE computer models and other recent studies reveal severe limitations in forecasting the benefits of liberalisation (Ackerman, 2005). Forecasting the impact of services liberalisation is even more difficult because, unlike trade, tariffs and quotas play a small role in service industries and the GATS negotiations do not focus on 'percentage reductions of well-defined, quantitative trade barriers' (ibid).

Models assessing the effect of the liberalisation of services have produced two widely different estimates of $53 billion (full liberalisation) and $427 billion (one third liberalisation) (Francois et al, 2003 and Brown et al, 2002). Ackerman concludes that 'a prudent conclusion might be that there is no solid basis for ... estimation of the benefits of services liberalisation at this time'.

Full global trade liberalisation figures are estimated to be between $84 billion – $287 billion, with the liberalisation of agriculture accounting for the bulk of benefits, and 85% of the benefits accruing to developed countries (ibid). The poverty reduction impacts are small ranging from 0.3% to 3.4% of global poverty using the $2 per day poverty line. Ackerman cites a study by Weisbrot et al that 'poverty reduction' may suggest a qualitative transformation in economic circumstances but the liberalisation models 'more often imply a change of pennies per day, moving people from just below to just above \$2 – valuable to be sure, but incremental rather than transformative' (ibid).

The models are further limited because they do not take account of the effects of liberalisation on employment. 'Critical dimensions of the real-world impacts of trade on employment and growth are excluded by design, while detailed attention is focused on secondary economic effects' (Ackerman, 2005). The computer models assume fixed employment and cannot take account of a net loss or gain in employment nor the quality of jobs caused by liberalisation. Stiglitz and Charlton also refer to the same limitations in their critique of forecasting the benefits of trade liberalisation (Stiglitz and Charlton, 2004).

CHAPTER 3

How markets operate

Markets are claimed to have two main advantages. Firstly, that they are efficient distributors of resources. Secondly, market relationships impose a structure on social relations which is beneficial to society because it creates a common framework and operational rules.

This section examines the structure of markets, market failure and the myth of the perfect market, market games, markets for public services and the welfare state, and the inefficiency of markets.

Markets are not created overnight nor simply by legislation and regulation. They have to be constructed and must have willing participants. They are political as well as economic constructs or frameworks. They do not just appear – they need prospects of profitability, indicators of longevity, and rules and regulations. They require a change in public values and principles so that competition, economic efficiency and profit-making are valued more than social needs, social justice and sustainable development.

Marketisation and privatisation occur as a result of political decisions, they are not a result of some inevitable process. Markets are planned as an integral part of New Labour's version of modernisation.

The marketisation and privatisation of public services is more advanced in Britain than any other European country. Thus it has very important lessons for Europe given the liberalisation of public services in the planned Internal Market Services Directive.

The structure of markets

Markets require certain structures and conditions:
● A set of values and ideology which determine the relationships between participants.
● A mechanism for setting prices for goods and services within individual budget constraints.
● Risk and reward (profit) for service providers.
● A system of rules and regulations including a procurement and contracting process with low transaction costs, minimal cost of regulation and compliance with a degree of self- regulation. A legal environment is required which gives authority and legitimacy for how contracts and transactions are to be carried out.

● The protection of property and intellectual rights.

● Access to the market by private and voluntary sector companies and organisations as willing providers with low entry and exit costs. In other words, providers can enter and leave the market at relatively low cost.

● Most public services require continued financing by the state and users, so financial systems must be designed for public money to follow pupils and patients to schools and hospitals in either public, private or voluntary sectors.

● A symmetry of information and knowledge amongst users and transacting parties. In theory, sufficient information is accessible to enable users to make decisions – in reality access, time, experience, knowledge and negotiating skills vary significantly between service users. This will lead to the emergence of brokers and agents to advise service users.

● Minimal environmental and social regulations with low-level community responsibilities.

● Excess provision or supply over demand so that there is spare capacity to allow market forces to operate. Closure of poor performing schools and hospitals and opening of new facilities and new entrants to the market depending on demand and performance, not social needs.

● Market failure minimised – such as the breakdown in contractual relationships between client and contractor, between contractor and suppliers or between contractor and service users.

● A level of inequality of access, use and participation, which is socially and politically acceptable.

The myth of the perfect market

A 'perfect market' is a theoretical concept rather than a practical reality. Minor market failures occur on a regular basis. For example, private contractors sometimes fail to deliver the required standard of service and have their contracts terminated. A market may produce negative environmental impacts such as pollution caused by a production process or traffic flows. However, these failures can usually be resolved at relatively low cost by market participants or state regulation. There are four types of significant market failure.

Firstly, 'externality occurs when one party's actions impose uncompensated costs and benefits on another party.' For example, overuse of supply such as over-fishing seas or lakes, or environmental

41

pollution caused by congestion or simply market participants ignoring the knock-on effects of their activities. Markets cannot be created in many public goods because it is impossible or inefficient to exclude individuals from benefiting.

Secondly, major firms or suppliers, acting alone or collectively, can exercise market power by reducing production in order to keep prices at an artificially high level and thus produce higher profits. They may also wield market power as a result of political pressure and sympathetic regulatory agreements. Bribery and corruption are sometimes used to win contracts and deter new market entrants.

Thirdly, market failure can occur from inadequate or asymmetric information, which results in an unacceptable high level of social costs, and a distortion in information held by market participants may lead to inefficient resource allocation.

Finally, a natural monopoly may exist when a service can only be supplied at the lowest cost by limiting delivery to a single provider. For example, a local authority refuse collection service is cheaper when it is carried out by one provider. Subdividing collection between two or more providers, or allowing a free market with residents having a 'choice' of provider which they pay directly rather than to the local authority, would increase costs substantially and will be very inefficient.

Market discipline
The following letter in the *Financial Times* during the debate about the role of the private sector in the NHS sums up the position of the free marketers and privatisers:

> 'The government's plans for competition in primary and hospital care in the National Health Service can only work if public and private providers can renegotiate the pay and employment conditions of all their employees.
>
> Furthermore, if organisations fail, all staff including medical and nursing staff, should lose their employment and have to seek new jobs. Without such market disciplines, how can the NHS be made to 'act smarter' as Mr Blair requires.'

Prof Alan Maynard, Professor of Health Economics and Director of the York Health Policy Group, University of York, 1 February 2006

Once market systems are established, right-wing and vested business interests will constantly seek to embed market discipline throughout the public sector. As always, the ultimate aim is to drive down terms and conditions and to eliminate public provision from all but the unprofitable services.

Market games

Markets and competitive regimes encourage contractors to maximise their income. To do this they resort to 'gaming' techniques which exploit loopholes in payment systems, ineffective monitoring and inspection, contract variations, and focus on high income activities. Construction companies are adept at submitting claims for additional costs. In health, gaming includes:

● Up-coding – recording additional unnecessary diagnoses and procedures, or selecting the most expensive diagnoses.

● Discharge and readmission of patients to attract additional payments for a single spell.

● Inappropriate admissions (for example, from accident and emergency).

● Deliberately keeping patients in hospital for more than 48 hours to attract the full tariff.

● Misclassifying patients into specialist healthcare resource groups that are funded through separate arrangements (*Health Service Journal*, 13 October 2005).

● Patient dumping by not accepting severely ill patients or 'under-treating' them by limiting or withholding more expensive treatments.

Techniques used in other services include:

● Dividing work into batches to maximise income.

● Ignoring service failures which have low financial penalties – it is often cheaper to bear the financial penalties imposed for poor service than it is to employ staff to correct them or uphold standards.

● Exploiting vagaries of contract responsibilities by maximising use of variation orders for claims for additional work, weather and client delays.

● Maximising changes for increased demand for services and/or out of hours service provision.

● Parking – the non-treatment of harder to help clients.

● Selective admissions

The inefficiency of markets

Efficiency is a means to an end, it is not an end itself – 'it is not a goal, but an instrument to achieve other goals. It is not a value, but a way to achieve other values' (Stein, 2001). 'Efficiency is about how we should allocate our resources to achieve our goals, not what our goals should be' (ibid). Efficiency has no inherent value. Minimising the cost of administration is often cited as an objective, an end itself, and it becomes a target with percentage reductions (often justified or legitimated by claiming to transfer 'savings' to 'frontline services'). But efficient at what, for whom and how does 'increased efficiency' impact on the quality of service and strategic objectives? On that basis, health and education could be made more efficient by excluding patients with long-term illness and pupils with learning difficulties! Efficiency can only be considered in the context of the overall objectives and strategy of a service. The cost of administration and use/allocation of resources (the 'cost of doing business' in the private sector) can only be assessed in the context of these objectives and strategy.

Government and public services are often branded as being inefficient whilst the private sector is considered efficient. 'Much of the case for public private partnerships rests on the relative efficiency of the private sector. While there is an extensive literature on this subject, the theory is ambiguous and the empirical evidence is mixed' (IMF, 2004).

Competitive markets are promoted as the means of imposing discipline in the public sector to make it more efficient. Competition is supposed to force a 'race to the top' and impose sanctions on inefficient providers by forcing them to either restructure or face closure. Service users become shoppers as consumers of public goods rather than citizens with human rights.

Markets, as noted above, are never static. Vouchers, savings accounts and other mechanisms are promoted to extend competitive forces and consumer choice, whilst increasing the scope for user charges through 'added value' contributions to widen 'choice'. The transaction, regulation and financial cost of operating competitive regimes are rarely quantified let alone taken into account; nor are the public costs of labour market impacts, accountability and increasing inequality.

Efficiency drive fuels marketisation
A new efficiency drive was launched following the Gershon Review (HM Treasury 2004a) with government proposals to achieve £21.5bn savings by 2007/08 built into the Spending Review 2004 (HM Treasury, 2004b). This extends the marketisation process in a number of significant ways:

● It will encourage further commercialisation of the public sector as managers look to copy private sector organisational structures, business values and working practices to achieve efficiency gains.

● The focus on efficiency and productivity is likely to further erode public sector values and priorities and make productivity and savings targets the focus of performance management.

● Despite the 'freedom and flexibility', 'localism' and sustainable development rhetoric, Departmental Technical Efficiency Notes emphasize making better use of buying power at a national rather than local or regional level for goods and services.

● Since most services have already been reviewed under Best Value, many managers will argue that they should move directly to procurement in the belief that bigger savings can be achieved by outsourcing than by another review of services.

● There will be fewer in-house bids because senior managers will claim that the biggest efficiency gains and savings can be achieved by outsourcing and transferring the employment responsibility to the private sector. 'Why use our time and resources in another review to make 3% efficiency savings when we could achieve a 20% saving by outsourcing'. This will directly increase the percentage of services provided by the private sector and increase market share for companies.

Resources diverted into marketing and branding

The way in which marketisation drives privatisation was noted in Chapter 2, in particular, arms length companies seeking independence, markets spawning brokers and agents, and diversification into other services (see page 24). Public and private providers will be increasingly forced into advertising and marketing to attract pupils and patients. Promoting a brand, differentiating the 'offer', cultivating niche markets, will require a marketing strategy, management responsibility, the production of advertising and marketing materials and a marketing budget. There are also likely to be restructuring and organisational costs further down the line as public and private providers withdraw from some services and start up new ones.

Public goods

Public goods have two key properties. They are non-excludable (users cannot be excluded from consuming the goods) and non-rival (consumption by one user does not reduce the supply available to others). The classic example is a lighthouse – ships cannot be excluded from using the lighthouse and when one ship is using it, the use by other ships is not affected. Traffic lights are another example. It is not possible to charge for their consumption.

The lighthouse example is needed for human safety, environ-mental and other reasons, but the light cannot be marketised. Thus the state is required to provide the lighthouse because of market failure.

Local or national public goods include defence, law and order, public health, macro-economic management, roads, parks and open spaces. Global public goods are those with benefits which extend across borders, populations groups and generations (Kaul et al, 1999).

Many public goods, services and activities could, in theory, be privately provided, but not without social costs, subsidies, increased inequality, stringent regulations, and the likelihood of increased collusion and corruption. But the state could outsource the delivery of public goods, for example the operation and management of the lighthouse and the maintenance of traffic lights.

Positive and negative externalities arise from the activities of individuals, firms, organisations and states which result in benefits (education benefiting society) or damage (air or river pollution) but they do not bear the costs. The state plays a crucial role in minimising negative externalities and promoting positive externalities through taxation, regulation, monitoring and inspection, planning and the provision of activities and services. States have also acted to regulate monopolies and afford consumer protection in the provision of goods and services. There are two other key attributes to public goods; they suffer from under-provision, and policy is mainly determined by the nation state.

Global public goods
The neoliberalism and privatisation/marketisation agenda over the last twenty-five years has led to shifts in what are termed public and private goods. A 'triangle of publicness' provides a useful framework to access individual public goods and the public domain (Kaul and Mendoza, 2003). The three elements of the triangle are:
● The publicness, or participatory nature, of decision making on which goods to place in the public domain.
● The publicness, or equity, of the distribution of benefits.
● The publicness of consumption or how the use and benefits of a public good are available to all.

The UN has identified ten global public goods which are fundamental to the implementation of the UN Millennium Declaration. They include basic human dignity for all people, including access to basic education and health care; respect for national sovereignty and global public health, particularly communicable disease control. Global security, or put differently, a global public domain free from crime and violence, and global peace are also important. Global public goods cover the harmonisation of communication and transportation systems and the institutional infrastructure across borders to foster such goals as market efficiency, universal human rights, transparent and accountable governance, and harmonisation of technical standards. The remaining global public goods include concerted management of knowledge, including worldwide respect for intellectual property rights, concerted management of the global natural commons to promote their sustainable use, and the availability of international arenas for multilateral negotiations between states as well as between state and non-state actors (Kaul et al, 2003).

Are New Labour's markets different?

Are the characteristics of New Labour's markets in public services so distinctly different from other markets? It is important to make some general observations about the current level of marketisation of public services. Many public services are rooted in the locality and cannot be produced elsewhere or offshored (Whitfield, 2001).

● Services such as health, education, housing, criminal justice are at different stages of marketisation and commercialisation.

● Only information and communications technology services and management consultancy operate on a truly global basis.

● There are wide differences in the size and composition of these markets with some 'fragmented' in the degree to which private companies are gaining market share in separate segments of a service market, for example education, but are yet unable to provide a holistic or comprehensive service.

● The private finance initiative/public private partnership infrastructure market has facilitated alliances between companies and financial institutions and hence increased the internationalisation of financial, construction and services markets.

● Supply chains vary between services, with some having well-established supply chains, for example, the health sector's purchase of pharmaceutical drugs, whilst others are fragmented.

47

The reality is that New Labour is creating *market conditions* in public services which include most of the structural components of markets outlined earlier in this chapter. Service users (or consumers in market language) do not make decisions on prices which are initially fixed and controlled by the state. In theory, they are making decisions on quality of service, convenience and other criteria but not price. Most service users want, first and foremost, a good quality local service. In these circumstances, choice is largely irrelevant. However, other participants in the market will be operating on a price structure, and the possible introduction of brokers and agents in the market will also be operating within the price mechanism.

Some regulatory controls will work, others will not, and thus require new regulatory frameworks and possibly legislation. It will take time for schools to move to foundation and trust status. Many will not want do so. Implementation drag is a factor in most radical change in the public or private sector due to opposition. It will also take time to persuade, cajole and bribe parents, pupils, patients and service users to actively and enthusiastically participate in the choice agenda.

Marketisation is a long-term strategy. It is not simply a matter of creating an education market or a health market but ensuring that market conditions are established more widely so that markets interact and generate new market mechanisms. The private finance initiative is a good example. Having become embedded in the public sector, it has developed a secondary market and new private finance initiative derivatives in the NHS Local Improvement Finance Trust and Building Schools for the Future.

New Labour is dressing up choice as empowerment. But the real power in marketisation is gained by transnational companies and consultancies which provide services and, slowly but surely, take over the ownership of key public sector assets. The private finance initiative has never been simply an alternative method of financing infrastructure investment, but a longer term strategy by which the private sector will ultimately own/control the welfare state infrastructure *and* provide privatised core services (Whitfield 2001).

Stream of policy documents

Labour's modernisation agenda is underpinned by the four principles of high national standards and accountability, devolution and delegation, flexibility in employment, and choice and pragmatism in terms of who delivers (OPSR, 2002). But the government has produced a stream of vision statements, plans and proposals in the last two years as the speed of modernisation has been ratcheted up. Even the performance management framework is being rethought (see Table 5). The Treasury's Devolved Decision-Making Review concluded that the current performance framework 'fosters compliance rather than innovation.' It places too much emphasis on accountability to central government rather than the community, a focus on the extremes of performance, too few incentives to involve people, and 'is increasingly rigid, complex, process heavy and resource hungry' (HM Treasury/Cabinet Office, 2004).

The policy documents are littered with principles, partnerships and claims of sustainable communities. There is confusion between core and operational principles and between the principles which have underpinned public services and those required to implement the marketisation agenda. The Office of the Deputy Prime Minister has a national research programme, which has engaged many public sector academics in large contracts evaluating the local government modernisation agenda. The first 'meta-evaluation' report confused principles and mechanisms, for example, increasing choice and personalised services, introducing contestability, devolving power to the frontline, and decentralising services to neighbourhood level are cited as 'principles of public service reform' in one part of the report and as 'drivers' in another (Office of the Deputy Prime Minister, 2005a). Accepting these policies as principles of public service reform without challenge or criticism seems to be another indicator of the ideological mainstreaming of neoliberalism and marketisation.

It is also significant that many of the policy documents stress the importance of community participation. The 'Together We Can' civil renewal document contains headings such as 'power to the people' and 'empowerment does work' (Home Office, 2005). But there are few references to staff and trade union participation in community participation processes or in terms of improving the planning and design of services, despite a long track record of positive initiatives.

Of course, there has been no community participation over the content of the marketisation programme. The real purpose of the rhetoric is revealed in the following statement: '... *reform and modernisation of the public services will not be accepted as legitimate unless it is based on citizens' support*' (Office of the Deputy Prime Minister, 2005b).

Table 5: *Major modernisation policy statements since 2004*

Recent policy documents for the modernisation agenda
Devolving Decision Making Review (HM Treasury March 2004)
The future of local government: Developing a 10 year vision (June 2004, ODPM)
The NHS Improvement Plan: Putting people at the heart of public services (June 2005)
Efficiency Review and 2004 Spending Review (HM Treasury, July 2004)
Departmental Five-year Plans – sustainable communities, housing, education, health (ODPM 2005, DfES, 2004), DoH, 2004) Local transport authorities five year plans due March 2006. DEFRA Rural Pathfinders (Lancashire)
Independence, Opportunity, Trust: A Manifesto for Local Communities (Local Government Association, September 2004)

Securing Better Outcomes: Developing a new performance framework (HM Treasury, January, 2005)	Vibrant Local Leadership (ODPM January 2005)	Citizen Engagement, Neighbourhoods and Public Services: Evidence from Local Government (ODPM, January 2005)	Citizen Engagement and Public Services: Why-Neighbourhoods Matter (ODPM, January, 2005)	New Localism – Citizen Engagement, Neighbourhood and Public Services (ODPM, January, 2005)

Education White Paper 14-19 Education and Skills (February 2005)
Meta-Evaluation of the Local Government Modernisation Agenda: Service Improvement in Local Government (Martin and Bovaird, ODPM, March 2005)
Together We Can: People and Government, Working Together to Make Life Better, Home Office, (2005)
Independence, Well-being and Choice: Our vision for the future of social care for adults in England (March 2005) White Paper.
Commissioning a Patient-led NHS (August 2005)
Higher Standards, Better Schools for All: More choice for parents and pupils (October 2005) White Paper.
Health Reform in England: update and next steps (December 2005)
White paper on reform of community Health services (January 2006)
Education Bill (2006)

CHAPTER 4

The five-stage marketisation process

The first three chapters examined New Labour's commitment to marketisation, and showed how marketisation drives the neoliberal agenda and how markets operate. This chapter provides a framework by which marketisation can be more fully understood, assessed and counter strategies developed.

There are five key processes in marketisation (see page 7 and Figure 2):

- Commodifying (commercialising) services.
- Commodifying (commercialising) labour.
- Restructuring the state for competition and market mechanisms.
- Restructuring democratic accountability and user involvement.
- Embedding business interests and promoting liberalisation internationally.

Marketisation is multi-faceted and cross cutting, affecting all parts of the public sector.

Some modernisation policies cut across all five elements of the marketisation process. Building Schools for the Future is a good example. It demonstrates how newer policies and programmes have a significant impact within a particular service, but also a cross-cutting impact on other services and public bodies as a whole. The ramifications of such policies reinforce the need to adopt broad community/public service alliance responses (see Chapter 11).

The potential impact of Building Schools for the Future is examined under each of the five elements in the marketisation process. Of course, the impact will not be uniform across local government and will depend on the strategies adopted by individual local authorities, trade unions, community organisations and Building Schools for the Future consortia.

Commodifying (commercialising) services

- Extends the marketisation of educational services and widens the scope of facilities management.
- Opportunity for the private sector to extend asset management to all secondary schools, primary schools and potentially to the rest of the local authority.
- Local Education Partnership (LEP) gives the private sector a key role in developing an education vision, provision of educational

Figure 2: *The marketisation process*

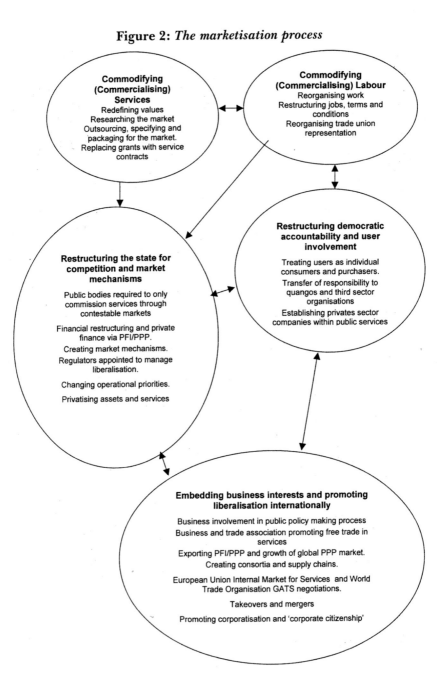

Commodifying (Commercialising) Services
Redefining values
Researching the market
Outsourcing, specifying and packaging for the market.
Replacing grants with service contracts

Commodifying (Commercialising) Labour
Reorganising work
Restructuring jobs, terms and conditions
Reorganising trade union representation

Restructuring the state for competition and market mechanisms

Public bodies required to only commission services through contestable markets

Financial restructuring and private finance via PFI/PPP.
Creating market mechanisms.
Regulators appointed to manage liberalisation.

Changing operational priorities.

Privatising assets and services

Restructuring democratic accountability and user involvement

Treating users as individual consumers and purchasers.
Transfer of responsibility to quangos and third sector organisations
Establishing privates sector companies within public services

Embedding business interests and promoting liberalisation internationally

Business involvement in public policy making process
Business and trade association promoting free trade in services
Exporting PFI/PPP and growth of global PPP market.
Creating consortia and supply chains.

European Union Internal Market for Services and World Trade Organisation GATS negotiations.

Takeovers and mergers

Promoting corporatisation and 'corporate citizenship'

services and entry into the policy making process.
● Local Education Partnership will help to drive Local Education Authorities into a commissioning role, which is the government's longer-term strategy.
● Local Education Partnershipss are almost certain to advise schools how to obtain trust or foundation status and provide services.
● Increases the range of 'additional services' because the Local Education Partnership could operate like a framework agreement in which the Local Education Authority and individual schools increasingly turn to it for advice, support and consultancy for a widening range of educational services.
● Direct Service Organisations may become unviable. Building Schools for the Future could then takeover provision of services to all schools.

Commodifying (commercialising) labour
● Extends staff transfer to a wider range of services.

Restructuring the state for competition and market mechanisms
● Establishes the Local Education Partnership as a commercial vehicle to create a new 'business' operating within the 'public sector'
● Building Schools for the Future is a key mechanism for delivering academies.
● Private finance of extended schools and new ICT services.
● New private sector investment in education will create new opportunities for the secondary market (refinancing of private finance initiative projects and the sale of equity in projects) and for capital accumulation.

Restructuring democratic accountability and user involvement
● Erodes democratic accountability, notwithstanding the role of the Strategic Partnership Board.

Embedding business interests and promoting liberalisation internationally
● Provides entry for private sector into education policy, children's services and educational information and communication technology.
● Consolidates the supply chain, further coralling teaching staff, and increasing capacity to bid for further Building Schools for the Future contracts.
● Building Schools for the Future is a means of extending opportunities for educational consultants to be part of private finance initiative consortia for the first time.

CHAPTER 5

Typology of marketisation
and privatisation

In the 1979-97 period, the Conservative government privatised the transport, energy, utilities and communications sectors, as well as most other nationalised industries and state-owned corporations. This period was dominated by the sale of assets through stock market flotations and trade sales (Whitfield 1992 and 2001). Three key areas remained in the public sector – the welfare state infrastructure, the criminal justice system, and defence. Labour commenced with a two-year commitment to the Tories spending plans and a rapid speed-up and widening of the role for the private finance initiative. Since then the modernisation agenda has consisted of a centralised performance management framework of targets and inspection, Best Value, mainstreaming procurement, strategic partnerships, outsourcing, the transfer of services to quangos and arms length companies, and a new efficiency drive.

The Labour government subsequently increased public spending, but modernisation has been rooted in a neoliberal ideology of competition and market forces.

New Labour has attempted to redefine privatisation, claiming it is limited to the sale of assets, and that marketisation is little more than the application of the principles of a mixed economy. The government has branded public private partnerships, strategic service-delivery partnerships (SSPs) and outsourcing as 'partnerships'. However, these policies involve the transfer of resources (staff, land, buildings, equipment, and intellectual capital) to private companies, private investment in the public infrastructure, and private management of a wide range of public services. This is privatisation.

New forms of marketisation and privatisation are constantly emerging. New private finance initiative/public private partnership models which include core services and more cross-cutting projects are likely to be developed. More formal organisational structures which divide strategic policy making and service delivery at local and regional levels are almost certain to develop in order to drive contestability across the public sector.

Marketisation is a key stage in preparing services for privatisation at a later date because they are too large for the financial markets and because of strong political opposition. Health, education and social

54

services have to be restructured, destabilised and fragmented into separate parts and corporatised to facilitate marketisation and, ultimately, privatisation. The financial markets could not cope with their privatisation by sale of assets and this is not a politically viable option.

Marketisation creates the conditions whereby full privatisation becomes inevitable:

● Competition and contestability imposes commercial values and operational systems on in-house services, often leading to the sale of direct service organisations.

● Encourages public sector arms length companies and trusts to expand and diversify, becoming more independent in the process, which in turn is used to legitimate full privatisation.

● Overstating the supposed needs of the 24/7 'customer service centre' whilst ignoring the other functions of the state. This leads to false divisions between front and back office functions and increasing the scale of the 'problem', and with insufficient in-house resources and capacity, leads to justifying the case for strategic partnerships with the private sector.

● Valorising public sector functions.

The effects of marketisation and privatisation have been detailed in Whitfield 1991 and 2001 and Florio 2004.

A typology of privatisation and marketisation
The typology of marketisation and privatisation provides a framework to explain and understand the different ways in which public services and the welfare state are being transformed. The different forms of marketisation do not take place in isolation. They are part of a broader restructuring of the state in the interests of capital.

There are four types of marketisation and privatisation of public services:

● Marketisation of global public goods
● Marketisation and privatisation of assets and services
● Privatisation of governance and democracy
● Privatisation of the public domain

The vertical columns in the typology identify the different forms of marketisation and privatisation, the methods used to further these policies, the political, social and economic objectives, and the impact on the state and public services.

Table 6: Marketisation and Privatisation Typology

Type of Marketisation and Privatisation	Method	Political, social and economic objectives	Impact on the state & public services
Marketisation and privatisation of global public goods			
Carbon market in response to climate change	Emissions trading system for greenhouse gases established under 1997 Kyoto Protocol. Polluter countries given 'emission credits' equivalent to 1990 level of emissions less their reduction commitment. Countries allocate credits on nationwide basis, most polluting industries receive biggest allocation. Polluters can buy and sell credits to other polluters on open market and invest in pollution reduction schemes in other countries to earn credits which can be used, sold or banked. Corporate-led self-monitoring and verifications schemes run by big business.	Retain business control with minimum commitments at minimum cost.	Large sums of public money required to establish trading system. Largely privatised system which is difficult to scrutinise.
Deregulation of protection of natural resources and the global commons	Privatisation of water and sanitation systems. Deregulation of environmental protection.	Attract inward investment and create new markets. Permit exploitation of minerals and natural resources with minimum controls.	Business claims ownership of natural resources and related property rights. Environmental degradation with knock-on effect on climate change.
Public health	Privatisation and commercialisation of health care systems including demands for trade and services liberalisation. Global Public Private	Creation of global markets. Harnessing public and private finance in Global Public Private Partnerships	Demise of health for all, segmentation and fragmentation of health care systems. Business

	…tnerships for specific diseases, drugs and vaccines.	…but remain under multilateral agency and commercial control.	dictate responses to diseases and epidemics.
Privatisation of global governance	Promotion of corporate citizen and corporate social responsibility (UN Global Partnership with business). Democratic accountability given low priority in development agenda.	Increase power of business and ensure business-friendly operating environment.	Fundamental lack of accountability of international agencies. Democratic accountability marginalised at national, regional and local levels.
Rise of privatised military industry	Outsourcing services and PPP projects for equipment for armed forces. Growth of private armies and security firms hired for civil wars.	Extending the military industrial complex beyond equipment and supplies to a wide range of services and functions.	Privately financed civil wars.
Marketisation and privatisation of assets and services			
Commissioning of public services from private and voluntary sectors.	Outsourcing and offshoring of services and/or transfer of work to the private sector. Adoption of commissioning role and withdrawal of public provision. Negotiating concordats with the private sector to deliver public services.	Reduce costs, abolish or regionalise national bargaining & increase productivity. Create new markets for private firms, weaken trade union organisation. Create competition between schools, hospitals and other services.	Decline in public provision and reduced state capacity.
Marketisation and expansion of private services, including franchising of services to the private and voluntary sectors.	WTO General Agreement on Trade in Services (GATS). European Internal Market in Services Directive. New Labour modernisation policies to create markets in provision of public services such as commissioning role	Creation/expansion of global and European markets in services. Mainstream contestability and competitive forces across the public sector. Restructure the role of the	Outsourcing of services and functions, commodification of of services and commodification of labour as staff transfer between contractors. Two tier

Type of Marketisation and Privatisation	Method	Political, social and economic objectives	Impact on the state & public services
	for health and social care and National Offender Management Service (NOMS) for probation and prisons. Marketisation process includes: 1. Commodifying services 2. Commodifying labour 3. Restructuring the state for competitions and market mechanisms 4. Restructuring democratic accountability and user involvement 5. Embedding business interests and promoting liberalisation internationally.	state from direct provision to making and sustaining markets.	workforce, equalities marginalised. State support for market through subsidies, tax concessions. Withdrawal/reduction of public services to spur private sector.
Private finance of infrastructure and services	PFI and PPP to design, build, finance & operate infrastructure and 'back-office' services. NHS Local Improvement Finance Trusts (LIFT) & Building Schools for the Future (BSF). Private sector sponsorship of Academy schools. Public and Community Interest Companies. Increased user charges and replacing grants with loans – students. Creation of a secondary market in selling stakes in PPP consortia and refinancing projects once operational.	Access to private capital and expertise. Legalised off-balance sheet financing of public investment.	Long-term financial commitment with private sector. Design, build, finance and operation by private contractors. Support staff transfer to private sector, longer-term threat to core services.
Choice and personali-	Competition between providers	Choice through competition	Fragmentation of public

	vouchers for services – child care and training.	create competitive pressure on 'failing' services. Promote middle class opting out.	...cilities such as schools and hospitals into separate stand-alone businesses to compete against each other.
Deregulation, liberalisation and re-regulation	GATS and European Union liberalisation and marketisation of services. Regulators appointed to deregulate and increase role of markets. Increased regulation of trade unions. Regulatory impact assessments to reduce obligations on business.	Create global markets in publicly funded services. Political cover provided by Regulators who operate 'independently' of government. Constrain trade union activity to oppose marketisation and privatisation.	Reduced power and capacity of state to intervene in markets. Market forces increasingly determine service provision. Increased competition and outsourcing.
Commercialisation of the public sector	Modelling public sector on private firm and organisation of services into business units operating with business values. Sponsorship of events. Public sector bodies urged to take on 'corporate citizen' and corporate social responsibility models the same as the private sector.	Market forces applied more widely across the public sector. Create conditions for further privatisation, marketisation.	Increasingly fragmented provision and internal trading. Business values gradually replace public service ethos.
Sale of assets to private sector through share flotations and trade sales	Sale of assets such as state owned companies, utilities, housing, land and property.	Extend property and company ownership. Income to enable tax cuts or maintain services which would otherwise be cut.	Asset stripping as sales undervalue public assets. Public sector responsible only for increasingly residualised services.
Sale and leaseback of government buildings	Public buildings and offices are sold with a long lease to a private investment company which in turn leases them back to the government or public body. Large number of government offices sold.	Fixing a price (valorising) of public buildings also extends the property market into public asset management. Also has short term financial benefits for public bodies.	Public sector loses direct control of the offices and buildings from which it operates.

Type of Marketisation and Privatisation	Method	Political, social and economic objectives	Impact on the state & public services
Asset Based Welfare	Child Trust Fund – vouchers issued to start savings schemes. Savings Gateway Individual Learning Accounts to access training.	Promotion of individual rather than collective responsibility for future social needs.	Encourage private suppliers and new markets thus marginalising state role to residual welfare state.
Increase domestic & family responsibility	Reducing scope of services and assuming family (women) take over responsibility for care of elderly & children. Separation of health and personal care.	Financial savings, promote family and social capital.	Service reductions and targeting. Means tested welfare state.
Privatisation of governance and democracy			
Contract governance	Mainstreaming national procurement policy across the public sector with larger and longer-term complex contracts. Partnership Boards and Joint Venture Companies run managed services contracts and Strategic Service-Delivery Partnerships. Wider use of management consultants for reviews, studies and procurement.	Separation of strategic policy making from service delivery. Establish organisational structures to extend contracting to wider range of services. Extend private markets by increasing outsourcing.	Loss of political control by elected members and erosion of democratic accountability and transparency. Growth of corporate welfare complex with a contract services system, owner-operator infrastructure industry, regulatory and financial concessions to business and the corporatisation of public bodies.
Transfer of services to arms length companies and corporatisation of quasi-public bodies	Foundation model for hospitals and schools which creates stand alone businesses. Formation of arms length companies for council housing (44 to date) economic	Increase business role in policy making process and delivery of services. Half-way to full privatisation at a later	Reduced range of direct publicly provided services. Reinforces 'enabling' model of the state. Loss of democratic

	...development and regeneration activities. Transfer of assets and services to third sector organisations such as housing associations and leisure trusts. Emergence of Local Public Service Boards which could takeover responsibility for services in Local Area Agreements. More central government quangos such as Partnerships for Schools and Partnerships for Health. Gated communities with 'self governance'	...date. Commodification of labour.	...accountability and transparency. Loss of provision of central and support services as transferred and corporatised bodies procure services from private sector.
Private companies established within public services	Building Schools for the Future – extension of PFI model to educational policy, provision of educational support services and build/operate schools through Local Education Partnership 80% controlled by private sector. Privately-run Academies in the school system.	Supplant role and function of Local Education Authority (LEA) which become commissioning bodies. Extend the role of the private sector in state education and marketise educational services.	Increasing marginalisation of LEA and run-down of in-house services. Loss of democratic accountability as privately controlled LEP has greater role in educational policy and provision. Parents, governors and teachers less influence in policy formulation.
Privatisation of development and regeneration responsibilities	Establishment of Urban Development (UDC) Corporations, Urban Regeneration Companies (URC) and Business Improvement Districts (BIDs) in city/town centres	Increase business involvement and influence in public policy making in growth and regeneration areas. Draw on business expertise and experience to speed-up development.	Erosion of democratic accountability, reduction in capacity of local government and public bodies. Business interests greater role in setting policy agenda.

Type of Marketisation and Privatisation	Method	Political, social and economic objectives	Impact on the state & public services
Privatisation of citizenship and political power	Focus on opinion citizens panels, polls & market surveys and 'armchair' voting. Community organising constrained by lack of resources.	Increase voter turnout to sustain legitimacy. Promote consumerism. Capacity building limited to aiding government policy implementation.	Users, community organisations and trade unions less involved in policy-making process. Centralised policies – localised involvement in marginal decisions – in effect community badging of central government policies.
Privatisation of public interest information – reduced transparency and disclosure	Widening scope of contracting and PPP's results in parallel use of 'commercial confidentiality' – much contract information exempt from Freedom of Information Act.	Protect commercial interest of the state and private capital.	Separation of policy and performance information/data. Makes scrutiny more difficult.
Privatisation of the public domain			
Public service values and principles being replaced by market ideology and commercial values	Extolling virtues and abilities of the private sector. Ignoring private sector failures. Creating 'no alternative' to private finance as economic orthodoxy.	Making market forces and the use of public resources to support them politically acceptable and reducing scope for opposition. Creating conditions for capital accumulation and profits from provision of public services.	Loss of legitimacy for in-house provision and increasing reliance on outsourcing and privatisation.
Privatisation of public intellectual capital	Extended use of consultants and Framework Agreements by public bodies.	Enable work to be carried out by either public or private sectors. TRIPS	Loss of knowledge of needs, the history and understanding of why

	WTO Trade-Related Intellectual Property Rights (TRIPS) – patents on products and processes for 20 years, protects monopoly rights. Nearly a fifth of known human genes have been patented – 63% owned by private biotechnology companies.	obliges governments not to disclose information of commercial value. Patents, knowledge, research, industrial designs and processes in private control and ownership.	things as they are. TRIPS hinders knowledge and technology transfer. Misallocation of public funds to corporate marketing, R&D focused on market/profit potential, not public social/health needs.
Privatisation of public space and domain	Extended use of consultants and Framework Agreements by public bodies. WTO Trade-Related Intellectual Property Rights (TRIPS) – patents on products and processes for 20 years, protects monopoly rights. Nearly a fifth of known human genes have been patented – 63% owned by private biotechnology companies.	Increase safety for middle classes. Respond to business interests in the cities.	More private control of 'public' spaces and activities in cities restricting protest and limiting activities.

Source: Developed from Public Services or Corporate Welfare: The Nation State in the Global Economy, Dexter Whitfield, Pluto Press, London, 2001.

CHAPTER 6

The marketisation process

This chapter examines in detail how the five elements of the marketisation process are implemented. Each section is organised around the headings in the chart in Chapter 4.
● Commodifying (commercialising) services
● Commodifying (commercialising) labour
● Restructuring the state for competition and market mechanisms
● Restructuring democratic accountability and user involvement
● Embedding business interests and promoting liberalisation internationally

Commodifying (commercialising) services

In-house services have to be restructured and repackaged if they are to be subjected to competition and delivery by the private or voluntary sector. Each service, groups of services or parts of services must be decoupled from other services so that they can stand alone with clear standards and responsibilities, and ultimately with their own bar-code.

The private delivery of public goods requires that their operational values, organisation structure and management systems be amended to suit those prevailing in the private or voluntary sector. Services have to be specified, including setting standards so that they can be priced, operate independently from other in-house or contracted services, and identify client and contractor responsibilities. The ownership of assets (equipment, buildings, depots, furniture) must be clearly established so that contracts can specify transfer of ownership or detail leasing responsibilities; for example, how equipment will be maintained over the contract period. Fragmentation leads to a loss of oversight and interconnectedness.

Redefining values
● Language of the market (contestability, contracting, commissioning, competition, choice, charging) replaces public sector values and principles (community needs, effectiveness, democratic accountability and the public interest). It promotes the view that it is acceptable for education, health and social services to be profit-making activities.
● Language and terms are used which are ideologically confusing, vague, evasive and often deceptive. For example, 'retaining the NHS

free at the point of use' could mean that the NHS is funded by the state but delivered by the private sector.

Pressure to accept 'reform' agenda
● Carrots and sticks – funding regimes are made conditional if local authorities and public bodies agree to implement national policies which accelerate marketisation and private sector involvement in the finance and delivery of services. Demands for efficiency savings are another stick to require procurement and outsourcing.
● Public sector organisations are required to have corporate commissioning and procurement policies and procedures by national performance management regimes which are regularly inspected/assessed.
● Separation of strategic policy making from service delivery.

Researching the market
● Private firms are consulted about their preference on the size and scope of contracts (via public sector open days, workshops, questionnaires, informal meetings between officers and company directors and contract managers).
● Market analysis identifies private sector provision, profiles of key companies and the level of interest in delivering public services. This process may include a 'market sounding' to determine the level of private sector interest.
● Encouraging voluntary organisations and social enterprises to bid for public service contracts.

Examples
Open days for potential bidders: Private contractors, construction companies, financial institutions and consultants are often invited to open days to present the project and encourage firms to bid. These events also allow the private sector to inform the authority about what the market expects in the specification, packaging and project design. Achieving a suitable level of 'market interest' may well conflict with the social and economic needs of the project and community.

Inviting bidders to extend scope of the contract: Pre-Qualification Questionnaire (PQQ) and Pre-Invitation To Negotiate (PITN) are issued by public bodies after a contract has been advertised in the Official Journal of the European Union and are used to question bidders technical ability and capacity in more detail. But they may also be used to determine whether contractors are interested in delivering the same service(s) across the authority as a whole, widening the scope of the contract to include other services, or providing services on a sub-regional basis by implying that other authorities may be interested in joining in the contract.

'Stimulating markets': The National Procurement Strategy for Local Government requires authorities to 'stimulate markets and encourage competition' by producing a selling-to-the-council guide, developing supply chain partnerships, preparing a concordat with small and medium sized businesses, and a compact with the voluntary and community sector. However, there is a fine line between promoting traditional council contracts for goods and services and 'stimulating markets' as a result of perceived pressure from current modernisation ideology, inspection regimes and business interests.

Creating and making markets: Government departments are encouraged to 'open discussions with industry well in advance about future requirements', obtain a view about 'the right number and nature of suppliers to support effective competition and security of supply', and to 'adjust demand and/or stimulate supply' when necessary (Office of Government Commerce, 2003).

'Dating Seminars': Partnerships for Schools is to host 'dating seminars' for architects and contractors in the next round of Building Schools for the Future in an attempt to bring down bid costs and to 'create a market around the BSF programme' (*Building*, 13 December 2005). This is another use of language being used to belittle the significance of the impact of such a process.

Outsourcing – specifying and packaging for the market
● Specifying the service so that it can be tendered and included in a contract.
● Packaging the service – identifying and separating the service from other functions so that it can be tendered individually or as a group of services.
● Identifying publicly owned assets such as equipment, buildings and land leased or owned by the service.
● Reviewing the cost of corporate support services such as payroll, human resources, legal and financial services, cleaning, repairs and maintenance.
● Increased use of management consultants to prepare for competition, organisational change, financial structuring and creation of a contracting culture.

● Private sector contracted to manage 'failing' public services or facilities, for example, Local Education Authorities, individual schools and hospitals – both Labour and Tory governments have used criticism of 'failing' schools and hospitals to impose a 'reform' agenda.

● Adjusting standards and targets for the private sector, for example the number of hip operations for the elderly rather than good quality geriatric care, which is much harder to quantify.

● Benchmarking with private sector and other public bodies but not taking account of the different organisational, financial and operational differences between public and private sectors.

● Annual procurement review programme in every local authority to assess performance, options and identify services which should commence the procurement process.

● The government has extended the competition model for new initiatives, policies and funding streams requiring public sector organisations to compete for resources.

● Individual facilities such as schools and hospitals become business organisations trading their service, which also requires them to procure their own services instead of centrally from the local authority or NHS.

● A client/purchaser/commissioning function is established with responsibility for promoting the creation of markets and private provision (they become advocates and 'managers' of the market). This is based on a belief that publicly delivered services are less efficient than the private sector and cannot innovate to the same extent (attributed to 'vested interests', mainly trade union resistance and poor management).

● Closure, withdrawal or rundown of in-house services, or turning them into business units with commercial values and operating business practices.

Examples
Packaging back office services for 'partnership' contracts: Information and communication technology, financial, human resource, legal and transactional services such as revenues and benefits are packaged into a single contract. Some authorities advertise a very broad range of services and then narrow the scope after seeing what the private sector wants and can deliver, for example Milton Keynes advertised virtually all council services before reducing the scope of the partnership contract with HBS Business Services.

Packaging services for private interests: Many local authority procurement policies require managers to consider 'deconstructing the service' if the market response to 'testing the market' does not draw sufficient response from the private and voluntary sectors.

Mainstreaming procurement: National Procurement Strategy in local government, launched in 2003 with a 3 year implementation programme (Office of the Deputy Prime Minister and Local Government Association, 2003). A similar national procurement strategy for the Fire and Rescue Service was launched in 2005 (Office of the Deputy Prime Minister, 2005).

Outsourcing in different sectors: There is little evidence of the current level of outsourcing of central and local government and NHS services. Procurement data often do not separate goods and services. The available data from Compulsory Competitive Tendering in local government and market testing in the NHS and central government is now out of date. An NHS survey revealed £2.3bn of services procurement with £795m outsourced (NHS PASA, 2003). See Table 10 for further details.

Private sector contracted to manage 'failing' services: Several Local Education Authorities – Bradford, Walsall, Leeds, Waltham Forest, Haringey – have had different levels and types of private sector management imposed by the Department for Education and Skills ranging from reviews by management consultants to private sector management, and in the case of Leeds, an arms length company managed by Capita.

Only one NHS hospital, the Good Hope Hospital in Sutton Coldfield, was managed by a private sector company, although several others have had NHS management support.

Commissioning could be outsourced: Thames Valley Strategic Health Authority decided to outsource the commissioning of healthcare for the Primary Care Trusts in Oxfordshire (*Financial Times,* 13 October 2005). 'Following informal discussion with key local stakeholders the Strategic Health Authority wishes to seize the opportunity presented by *Commissioning a Patient Led NHS* and the increasing culture of developing choice and plurality in the NHS by exploring the opportunity of extending plurality to the management and delivery of the commissioning function' (Board Paper 62/05, Thames Valley SHA, 12 October 2005). Although the procurement process did not start after a Health Minister expressed opposition, it clearly shows the intent and the outsourcing of commissioning is likely to arise again.

Strategic Partnerships with private sector: About 20 local authorities have a Strategic Service-delivery Partnership (SSP), essentially a large long-term multi-service, multi-million pound outsourcing contract with a private contractor. Normally between 100 and 1,000 staff in information and communications technology, financial services, human resources and property management transfer to a contractor (for example BT, HBS business Services, Vertex, Capita). Staff are seconded in a few contracts. Some Partnerships have substantially expanded the range of services they provide.

Shared services: The concept of shared services or shared business centres is a key part of the Gershon efficiency agenda. A few local authorities are sharing the provision of corporate and transactional services via informal arrangements, one authority providing services for neighbouring authorities or via Joint Venture Companies. Others are planning strategic partnerships and outsourcing.

NHS Shared Business Services (SBS) is a joint venture with Xansa, the outsourcing and technology contractor with centres in the UK and India. SBS provides financial, accounting and payroll services to primary care trusts and trusts with £30m investment from the Royal Bank of Scotland.

Government competitions for pilots and pathfinders: The Government frequently does not wait for the evaluation of pilots and pathfinders before mainstreaming policies across all local authorities and public bodies as, for example, with Local Area Agreements.

Concordat with private sector: A concordat was signed in 2000 to provide up to 150,000 procedures purchased per annum. It also provided for private sector management to run 'failing' NHS Trusts, the formation of joint ventures between the NHS and private sector, and provision of intermediate care in nursing homes and the community (Department of Health Press Release 0629, 31 October 2000).

Transferring services to private sector treatment centres: The NHS Treatment Centre programme was divided into NHS and privately-run centres. The Department of Health commissioned 530,000 operations from 34 private sector-run Treatment Centres plus two supplementary contracts for 9,000 orthopaedic patients. The government has guaranteed patient volumes and the private sector's start-up costs are recognised in the pricing structure. If patients chose not to use the private treatment centres resulting in under-utilised resources, the private sector still gets paid under the guaranteed volume agreement.

The NHS Improvement Plan stated that the private sector 'may' provide up to 15% of NHS operations by 2008, in effect confirming an earlier statement by the then Health Secretary John Reid that the private sector would carry out 'a maximum of 10-15 per cent' of NHS operations (NHS Improvement Plan, 2004 and Health Service Journal 20 January 2005).

An independent assessment of the first six months performance of five providers (Nuffield, Capio, Netcare, Partnership Health Group and Birkdale Clinic covering mixed activity, orthopaedics and ophthalmology) concluded that the variation in data collection and completeness of the Key Performance Indicators (KPI) in the contract 'renders any attempt at commenting on trends and comparisons between schemes and with any external benchmarks futile ... We have felt constrained in making any judgments on performance ... We have no way of judging the accuracy of the data submitted and have to take them at face value. We recommend independent validation through sample audits against case notes.' (National Centre for Health Outcomes Development 2005).

Management of NHS Treatment Centres outsourced: The management of some NHS-run Treatment Centres may be outsourced in the £3bn second wave contracts for a further two million operations announced in May 2005.

Primary Care Trusts forced into 'take or pay' with private sector: Primary Care Trusts contracts with privately-run Treatment Centres are on a 'take or pay' basis which has meant they have been forced to reduce elective surgery at NHS Trusts. This has led to financial deficits and cuts for NHS Trusts. In effect the government's national procurement programme for Treatment Centres is substituting NHS services with private sector healthcare. 79% of chief executives in a Health Service Journal and NHS Confederation survey of 63 primary care trusts and 48 acute trusts stated that they had been required to reduce activity or forgo growth by the national procurement programme.

Outsourcing of NHS Walk-in Commuter Centres and GP surgeries: Seven new NHS walk-in centres for commuters are planned at Liverpool Street, Canary Wharf, Kings Cross, Victoria, Leeds, Manchester Piccadilly and Newcastle rail stations. The Department of Health invited private sector bids 'to increase the range of primary care provision' (DH Press Release 04/2005). Only two have opened to date, Manchester Piccadilly and Liverpool Street, operated by Atos Origin and General Medical Clinics, respectively. Atos Origin is a transnational ICT and managed services company operating in 40 countries.

UnitedHealth Europe was recently appointed preferred bidder to run two GP practices in Derbyshire and announced it plans to establish 'super-surgeries' across the UK over the next five years. A pilot scheme for a 'wave' of new GP practices and walk-in centres was launched by the Department of Health in July 2005. Contracts have not yet been awarded.

The combination of these projects and the shift of resources primary care, coupled with the Department of Health's commissioning agenda, will create vast new opportunities for the private sector to become firmly embedded in NHS provision.

Trust and Foundation status for schools and hospitals: The combination of establishing a trust or company status with the severing of the central supply of support services, together with the capacity to own their own buildings and employ their own staff, requires the redesign of support services for procurement from the private sector.

Clinical services may be included in future NHS Local Improvement Finance Trust (LIFT) projects – Partnerships for Health has been examining this possibility and canvassing private healthcare companies, which not surprisingly, expressed 'significant interest' (*Health Matters No 60*, Summer 2005). The clinical services mentioned include essential medical services, replacement of additional services (for example, cervical screening, child health surveillance services, maternity medical services and minor surgery), enhanced services (for example, more specialised services for patients with multiple sclerosis, more specialised sexual health services, provision of intermediate care), and out-of-hours services.

Replacing voluntary organisations' grants with contracting for services
● Grants for activities and services provided by community groups and voluntary organisations terminated and replaced with a contract.
Example
Voluntary sector capacity building to bid for public sector contracts: Government launches capacity building programme with £125m funding and encouragement to persuade voluntary and community organisations and social enterprises to bid to take over provision of public services. Future Builders: £125m funding to increase the capacity of voluntary organisations to bid for public service contracts.

Commodifying (commercialising) labour

The commodification or commercialisation of the workforce engaged in delivering the service runs parallel to the commodification of the service. Commodifying labour means changing the organisation of work and staffing levels to more precisely meet the requirements of the commodified service – job descriptions, terms and conditions, grading structures and staffing levels are geared solely to the delivery of the service. The aim is to get a close match between the basic needs of the service with the minimum possible wage and operational costs. Support services are re-negotiated through Service Level Agreements to achieve the minimum required level of service at the lowest cost. In the European Union, the Acquired Rights Directive provides for the transfer of staff to a new employer when services are outsourced, providing that the service is an economic entity.

Reorganising work
● Reorganising the service delivery process by separating different functions so that they can be supplied at the lowest possible cost.
● Changing the organisation of work, working practices and adoption of 'operating to contract' approach.
● Separating 'front line' and 'back office' functions to identify the minimum skills, training and professional responsibilities required for each function.
● Adjusting job descriptions to working practices and responsibilities so that skill levels, job descriptions and pay rates are matched with minimum staffing levels (optimising the way tasks are performed, simplifying jobs to minimise skills, training and wages).
● Making staff more transferable between employers. TUPE regulations provide a degree of protection for staff, but also enable them to be transferred to a new employer. It severs the relationship between public service provision and in-house delivery.
● Rewards of career progression for staff who take up the modernisation mantle.
● Limiting debate and the ability to challenge the implementation of modernisation policies, and branding those proposing alternatives as 'dinosaurs' and 'obstructers of change'.

Examples
Best Value and efficiency reviews: Service and efficiency reviews, options appraisal and threat of procurement or transfer to arms length company

creating insecurity for public sector staff who made conscious decision to work in the public services. Often carried out by management consultants. Reviews frequently recommend closing facilities, reducing the level of in-house provision, or withdrawing services.

New efficiency and productivity reviews: Service reviews which focus on changing work processes to reduce costs to meet efficiency targets.

Restructuring staffing: The combination of public private partnerships/private finance initiative projects, commissioning and outsourcing services will lead to a reduction in workload in corporate services resulting in further rationalisation. Staffing levels in catering, cleaning and other services are frequently redesigned with rotas to reduce working hours below National Insurance Rate lower limits to avoid employer costs.

'Fitness for Purpose' reviews: A combination of commissioning and cuts strategies leads to organisational and financial reviews, which may lead to mergers of public sector bodies and withdrawal from service delivery, for example the review of Primary Care Trusts launched in autumn 2005.

TUPE regulations and Code of Practice on Workforce Matters: Two-tier workforce in local government prohibited from March 2003 and other public services since March 2005. The Code does not apply to contracts agreed before these dates. The Code applies across the public sector but this is as much a concession to the private sector by guaranteeing the transfer of skilled labour and reducing opposition to procurement, outsourcing and partnerships as it is a concession to trade union demands. However, the legislation has a dual function – it affords workers greater protection but also facilitates easier transfer of staff between employers.

Restructuring jobs, terms and conditions
● Intensified competition between workers as information and communication technology-related work can be offshored.
● Watering down of pension provisions, which reduces quality differentials between public and private sectors.
● Increased use of agency staff and temporary workers.
● Schools and hospitals operating as businesses require a company secretary, chief finance officer and business managers whose relatively high wages are used to justify pay increases for other senior management.
● Key specialists or senior staff with expertise, reputation and/or

research grants are 'traded' between universities, hospitals and new 'centres of excellence'.

● Key staff sent on business planning, procurement training, private finance initiative/public private partnership and management courses, and attend 'modernisation' conferences frequently organised by the private sector and dominated by a business agenda.

● Focus on entrepreneurialism in recruiting new staff, particularly business managers, often from the private sector, to head public sector organisations and business units.

Examples

Big wages increases for senior managers: Chief executives of arms length management organisations received substantial pay increases compared to the previous Director of Housing, for example in Newcastle and Ashfield. Arms length companies require the appointment of a Company Secretary whose salary is often used to justify pay increases for other senior staff. New stand-alone organisations or companies such as Foundation hospitals and schools, arms length management organisations and leisure trusts hire entrepreneurial managers to head up their commercial operations.

Terms and conditions: Many contractors are claiming that their terms and conditions are 'reasonably similar' to those in the public sector in the application of the Best Value of Practice on Workforce Matters.

Two–tier pensions schemes: Most private contractors operate separate pension schemes for transferred staff and new starters, the latter usually being lower quality money purchase schemes.

Revolving doors: Senior civil servants, local authority and NHS officers are recruited by private contractors. One minute they have responsible public sector jobs, the next minute they are working for the private sector who rely on exploiting their inside knowledge.

Casualisation: Creating small core and peripheral workforces of temporary and casualised staff. This practice is widely used in leisure, catering, and community care where there are substantial differences between public and private sector wages.

Reorganising trade union representation

● Fragmentation of trade union organisation as outsourcing and transfer of functions to arms length companies increases the number of employers and private contractors seeking to impose their own practices.

● Staff and trade union participation in Best Value is reduced to consultation at specific stages of the review and options appraisal process.
● Trade union rights are curtailed, and their ability to influence the policy agenda is weakened.
● Applying information and communications technology to the way the service is delivered – this can benefit the service and staff but it may also impose new constraints on the way staff work and implies more intensive monitoring.

Example
Private contractors and arms length companies: frequently limit trade union representation to staff directly employed by the company. This may result in less experienced representatives and weaker trade union organisation.

Restructuring the state for competition and market mechanisms

The formation of markets and competition or contestability require changes in the role of the state, the organisation of service delivery, and the financing of public provision. Client and contractor roles are separated, and financial systems are changed so that public money follows patients and pupils. The establishment of arms length companies and trusts for some services forces them to operate as commercial stand-alone organisations.

Public bodies required only to commission services through contestable markets
● Government launches 'fit for purpose' reviews of the functions and objectives of public service organisations when it wants to change their remit to 'strategy and commissioning', meaning imposing competition, procurement and outsourcing.
● Framework Agreements operate with either one or three or more contractors, selected through a procurement process, who are then allocated work as and when required through a call-down system. A Framework Agreement with a single contractor means that there is no requirement to tender work for the period of the agreement, normally four years, and projects are negotiated and a price agreed. 'Mini competitions' are sometimes held for projects where there is more than one contractor in the Agreement – there is no requirement to re-run the procurement process. Contractors in the framework

agreement submit costed proposals which are assessed by the client.
● Commissioning is another name for client responsibilities which
range from defining, identifying and assessing needs, understanding
the market, specifying services, managing the procurement process
and negotiating contracts, monitoring and contract management, and
evaluating policy and regulatory frameworks. Shift from micro-
commissioning (for individuals) to regional commissioning driven by
the pressure for efficiency savings.

Examples
National Procurement Strategy for Local Government requires
mainstreaming of commissioning and procurement procedures with
training, new procurement teams, and cabinet committees in 2003-
2006 action programme (Office of Deputy Prime Minister and Local
Government Association 2003).

National Offender Management Service (NOMS): NOMS combines the
prison and probation services into one organisation. The NOMS
Strategic Business Case identifies key work areas which include a
switch to commissioning, 'performance testing' of prisons where they
are challenged to improve or are market tested or contracted out,
market testing of probation services, and future investment and estate
rationalisation to increase competition and a wider range of suppliers.
'The market in NOMS community services is less well developed and
we will devise a targeted market testing strategy to improve quality
and value for money' (National Offender Management Service, 2005).

The NOMS Offender Management Model is built around an
offender-focused human service approach to work with individual
offenders with a single concept of sentence implementation. The 'one
sentence-one manager' structure is a brokerage approach in which an
offender manager brokers resources but does not commission or
purchase them. Ten Regional Offender Managers (ROMS) will work
across both services to commission services which 'will dramatically
increase the level of contestability in the system' (ibid).

Primary care 'fitness for purpose review': Reorganisation and reduction
of to deliver £250m savings via a 15% cut in management costs,
reducing the number of Trusts from 303 to less than a hundred.
Primary care trusts were originally required to become
commissioning-only bodies by December 2008, with up to 250,000
staff facing transfer to a new employer as services are transferred to
other providers when the government 'opens up the primary care

market' (Department of Health, 2005). However, the government were forced to retract this requirement and timetable but clearly this remains an objective.

Community care commissioning and TUPE avoidance: Many local authorities systematically reduced in-house provision of social care by using 'spot contracts', in other words using 'commissioning officers' to drip feed individual care packages to the private and voluntary sector rather than using 'block contracts' as staff left or retired. This avoided a TUPE transfer of staff since individual care packages do not legally constitute an 'economic entity'. Since no staff were transferred, there was no obligation on private and voluntary sector providers to maintain local authority terms and conditions.

Competitive tendering in legal aid: The Lord Chancellor announced plans in July 2005 to force solicitors to compete for legal aid work via block contracts with a smaller number of firms. Lord Carter, famous for prison privatisation and National Offender Management Service marketisation, has been asked to carry out a review of how the government purchases legal aid. 'Lord Carter of Coles will produce a plan to use modern procurement methods to contribute to a more proportionate way of spending legal aid while ensuring reasonable client choice and sufficient quality' (Department of Constitutional Affairs, Press Release, 5 July 2005).

Market in higher education: Following the decline in student numbers in mathematics, chemistry, chemical engineering, metallurgy and materials engineering and information and technology and systems science, followed by the closure of some university centres, a Higher Education Funding Council for England (HEFCE) working group concluded that 'HEFCE should guard against an overtly interventionist role in the market. The Council should be wary of preventing the natural development of disciplines or infringing institutional autonomy or academic freedom. Second-guessing the market may ultimately reduce the dynamism of the English HE sector' (Higher Education Funding Council for England, 2005).

Diagnostics healthcare market: The NHS signed a five-year £80m contract with Alliance Medical for 130,000 Magnetic Resonance Imaging (MRI) scans per annum. But in the first year 70,000 paid-for scans were unused (*Health Service Journal,* 18 August 2005). Bridgepoint Capital, Alliances's parent company, also owns Tunstall telecare systems and two nursing and residential home operators.

Partnership for Schools Framework Agreement: This covers seven areas such as technical advice, education policy, project management, financial and legal services. Local authorities with Building Schools for the Future projects can commission work from the companies selected by Partnerships for Schools through a procurement process. It operates like an 'approved list' and ensures that local authorities obtain the 'right' kind of advice approved by Partnership for Schools (PfS, 2005).

Financial restructuring and private finance via
private finance initiative/public private partnership

● Distribution of resources switched from area/population social needs basis to follow pupils and patients and 'payment by results'. The financial viability and economic needs of corporatised public bodies, essential to make the market work, are prioritised over public service needs. Bonus payments are often introduced to encourage increased patient/pupil volumes for particular services. This distorts service delivery, as public organisations become more commercially orientated and business-like, focusing on 'profitable' work streams at the expense of other activities. It can result in over-supply, over-diagnosis and over-treatment.

● Private finance – Labour's first Act of Parliament in 1997 was to clarify the legal basis of the private finance initiative/public private partnerships and to initiate and implement the Bates Review on how the private finance initiative could be speeded up.

● Subsidising the set-up costs of the private sector so that they can compete with public services. Private sector given guarantees of volumes of NHS patients and their start-up costs taken into account for an initial period.

● Decoupling public funding from public provision – increasing emphasis placed on public finance of public services to maintain the 'free at the point of use' commitment, but this could mask a service provided entirely by the private sector. Continued public funding is only a partial guarantee.

● Introduction of insurance schemes, vouchers, savings schemes and financial incentives to encourage competition, choice and trading – personal 'top-ups' provide an additional fill-up for markets – and encourage a switch to an asset-based welfare system.

● Additional 'freedom and flexibility' reward to 'high performing' NHS Trusts and local authorities, but perversely allowing them to operate at arms length and become more business-like.

● Concealing or failing to identify the full cost of marketisation, regulating markets, commissioning and procurement (the transaction costs), ignoring the direct and indirect public impact (economic, social, health, equality, environmental and sustainable development) with the public sector bearing the cost of closure of schools and hospitals because of market forces.

● Research grants for investigating social needs and developing new services now have to compete against those assessing the plethora of modernisation initiatives.

Examples

Private finance initiative and infrastructure market: The Private Finance Initiative was launched by the Tories in 1992, but New Labour ensured it blossomed by extending its scope to education, housing, the criminal justice system, and defence, and embedding it as a major source of infrastructure funding. Table 7 summarises the £46.6bn signed private finance initiative deals in Britain. The 2005 Pre-Budget Report identified a further £11.6 billion capital value of private finance initiative projects currently at preferred bidder stage and expected to reach financial close by 2006/07. Health and Defence account for 45% and 36% of these projects respectively (HM Treasury 2005). There are also numerous projects at the planning stage.

The Department of Health has used the private finance initiative almost exclusively for NHS investment. 80 Prioritised Capital Schemes have been approved since May 1997 with a capital value of £17.2 billion plus 47 Non-Prioritised Schemes over £10m with a capital value of £1.2 billion. In contrast, just six publicly funded Prioritised schemes have been approved with a capital value of £500m plus another six non-prioritised schemes with a capital value of £117m (Department of Health, 14 December, 2005). Massive cost increases have plagued private finance initiative projects in the NHS. The capital costs of twenty-two schemes increased an average 117% between the original capital cost at the Outline Business Case and the latest capital value in 2005 (Department of Health table in Reform, 2005).

NHS Local Improvement Finance Trust (LIFT): LIFT is a £1bn programme to renew the primary care and social services infrastructure such as GP surgeries, health centres and one-stop-centres. It has a different structure from 'normal' private finance initiative schemes. The Department of Health and Partnerships UK

Table 7:
Signed private finance initiative projects in UK

Service	No of projects	Value of projects (£m)
Education		
Primary schools	19	221
Secondary schools	59	1,653
Primary and secondary schools	59	2,633
Further education	20	210
Higher education	13	436
Sub-total	**170**	**5,153**
Health		
Hospitals and related facilities	168	6,150
District and community health	22	325
NHS LIFT	42	1,000
Sub-total	**232**	**7,475**
Housing	**12**	**490**
Criminal justice		
Courts	7	204
Police	21	369
Prisons	16	547
Sub-Total	**44**	**1,120**
Fire	7	83
Leisure	9	122
Libraries	7	72
Government and local authority offices and property	40	2,599
Transport		
London Underground	8	17,363
Transit systems, terminals and interchanges	10	1,342
Roads	24	3,078
Street lighting	11	273
Sub-total	**53**	**22,056**
Defence		
Barracks	8	768
Equipment 20 1,028		
Sub-total	**28**	**1,796**
Information technology (all departments)	82	3,690
Water, waste and environment	28	1,674
Energy	14	117
Misc and equipment all services	22	153
Total	**744**	**46,600**

Source: PartnershipsUK database accessed 12 January 2006.

(51% owned by the private sector) established a national joint venture company, Partnership for Health, which facilitates local joint ventures (LIFTCos), in which the private finance initiative contractor has a 60% stake with Partnerships for Health and local stakeholders (usually Primary Care Trusts) each having a 20% stake. LIFTCo builds and refurbishes premises which it leases to primary care trusts, general practitioners, dentists, pharmacists and social care/voluntary organisations (see page 71 for inclusion of clinical services in LIFT projects). LIFTCo batches projects in an area in order to meet the minimum £20m capital cost imposed on private finance initiative projects. It also has an exclusivity agreement for future projects over the 20-25 year contract, which are determined by a strategic plan prepared by a Strategic Partnering Board.

51 Local Improvement Finance Trust projects have been approved in four waves; 37 projects reached financial close by December 2005, with a further five at preferred bidder stage, and nine projects at an early stage of procurement, with a capital value of about £1bn. 'NHS LIFT gives investors a seat at the planning and not just the providing table' stated Alan Milburn, previously Secretary of State for Health in a speech to the Public Private Partnership Forum in 2004 (Milburn, 2004). Six consortia have won over half the 42 contracts awarded to date led by Excell Care (a joint venture between John Laing's Equion and the Bank of Scotland) and Global Solutions led by Babcock & Brown (Australian global infrastructure investment company). The LIFT rate of return – 14.3% to 15.9% – is higher than that obtained by other similar-sized private finance initiative projects (12.5% to 15.0%) (National Audit Office, 2005).

A National Audit Office study of the LIFT programme (NAO, 2005) 'is fundamentally flawed' because it is based on surveys of participants with a vested interest in LIFT schemes, and did not include comparisons with other financing methods, risk transfer, affordability or governance issues (Centre for International Public Health Policy, 2005).

Building Schools for the Future
Building Schools for the Future (BSF) is the government's new private finance initiative programme to renew the secondary school infrastructure in England over the next fifteen years. A Local Education Partnership (LEP), 80% controlled by the private sector, with the local authority and Partnership for Schools (a new

Department for Education and Skills quango) each with a 10% stake, is at the core of Building Schools for the Future.

The Local Education Partnership will design, build, finance and operate new and refurbished schools using a mix of public and private investment. But Building Schools for the Future is not just about the provision of new schools. The local education authority must fully review its educational vision, develop a strategy for educational provision which integrates the building programme with service delivery, a new information and communications technology infrastructure, teaching, school management and community use. Council's are being threatened that if they do not have at least one academy, then Building Schools for the Future funding will be withheld. The local educational partnership will not only deliver facilities management but also provide other services such as educational support services and school transport (see page 51 for analysis of the wider impact of Building Schools for the Future).

Global public private partnership market
Some US$260 billion has been invested globally, mainly in Europe, Australia and Canada, by the private sector in public private partnerships between January 1994 and September 2005 (Pcw, 2005). Projects in Europe in this period were valued at 1bn Euros, with the United Kingdom accounting for two thirds of the deals, and Spain and Portugal accounting for 9% – 10% each.

Telecoms accounted for nearly 50% of public private partnerships in low and medium income economies in the 1990-2004 period, according to the World Bank's public private partnerships database – see Table 8. Energy projects accounted for about a third of public private partnerships investment, followed by transport with 15%, and water projects a mere 5%.

Public private partnerships in Britain differ from the global norm in several key ways: they extend across the public sector, including the welfare state infrastructure, defence and criminal justice system, in contrast to public private partnerships elsewhere, which are concentrated in transport, energy and telecoms. A higher percentage of design, build, finance and operate contracts in Britain result in more extensive outsourcing of facilities management. A wider range of services are included in public private partnerships projects, and the Local Improvement Finance Trust and Building Schools for the Future provide opportunities to provide core services and a wider range of additional services. Secondary markets have emerged in Britain for refinancing of project debt and public private partnership equity disposals (contractors wanting to realise profits and recycle capital into new projects) together with pooled secondary funds by investment trusts.

Table 8:
Global public private partnership investment by region
1990-2004 (US $billion)

Region	Energy	Telecom	Transport	Water/ sewage	Total
Europe* & Central Asia	31.6	96.1	5.4	3.8	136.9
East Asia & Pacific	78.6	56.8	46.0	15.8	197.3
Latin America & Caribbean	122.8	167.5	63.3	21.0	374.6
Middle East & North Africa	14.0	25.6	2.2	0.2	42.0
South Asia	24.2	24.4	3.9	0.2	52.8
Sub-Saharan Africa	7.1	28.7	3.2	0.2	39.3
Total	**278.3**	**399.1**	**124.0**	**41.2**	**842.6**

Source: World Bank Private Participation in Infrastructure Database, 2005.
* Low and middle income countries only

The private sector may also bid to takeover existing sections of the infrastructure. For example, a consortia of road construction companies submitted a $1 billion bid in July 2005 to takeover the Dulles Toll Road, one of Northern Virginia's main commuter routes. The bid involves a 50-year private sector takeover of the management, maintenance and improvement of the road plus toll collection, which generated a $28.5m surplus in 2004/05. The State of Virginia would retain ownership of the road (*Washington Post*, 26 July 2005).

Government privatises private finance initiative advice unit: The Treasury taskforce on the private finance initiative, Partnerships UK PLC, was privatised by Labour in March 2001 via a 51% sale of shares. The Treasury and the Scottish Executive retain a minority holding of 44.6% and 4.4% respectively. Investors include private contractors Serco, Prudential Assurance, Sun Life Assurance, Abbey National, Royal Bank of Scotland, Barclays Bank, British Land, Uberior Infrastructure Investments, and GSL Joint Ventures have share stakes of between 8.8% and 2.2%.

Partnerships UK has a stake in Partnerships for Schools and Partnerships for Health

Large Scale Voluntary Transfer finance market: Over 130 local authorities transferring their council housing stock to new or established housing associations, financed by French, Canadian and other overseas financial institutions (*Social Housing*, 2004).

Guaranteeing volumes of private sector users: The Department of Health guaranteed patient volumes in the first £3 billion tranche of non-emergency operations carried out by private sector Independent Treatment Centres. Primary care trusts were forced to pay for activity that was not used. For example, 14 primary care trusts in Greater Manchester had to pay Netcare, a South African private health firm, £1.9m for 6,000 operations, yet fewer than 4,000 had been carried out (*Health Service Journal*, 15 December 2005). Ashton, Leigh and Wigan Primary Care Trust paid nearly £500,000 for 688 operations, but only 67 patients have been treated to date.

Subsidising the set-up costs of the private sector: The Department of Health paid a 15% premium on the cost of operations carried out by the private sector to take account of their set-up and investment costs and to attract foreign firms into Britain to build private sector healthcare capacity.

Private finance initiative supplement paid to some NHS Trusts: The introduction of the payment by results system led to some private finance initiative hospitals receiving less money than anticipated when the PFI deal was signed, so the Department of Health was forced to step in with a £45m 'supplement' to University College Hospital in London, with more payments likely for other private finance initiative hospitals (*Building*, 1 July 2005).

Financial incentives to promote choice agenda: Primary Care Trusts were offered a £95m 'bonus' if they offered patients a choice of hospital treatment through the Choose and Book scheme in 2005/06. The money will be paid in stages as GP practices installed computer systems to offer patients an electronic menu of choices.

Three-quarters of NHS patients wanted more say in their treatment but just 30% thought having a choice of hospital was important, according to a MORI survey commissioned by the Department of Health in 2004. Treating patients with dignity and respect and listening to their views were cited as other important priorities (*Guardian*, 6 April 2004).

Payment by Results (PbR): Payment for hospital treatment has switched from local negotiated block contracts to a national tariff of over 1,000 procedures each with a Health Resource Group code. Hospitals are paid only for operations and procedures performed. It forces hospitals to operate like businesses. If they perform an operation at less than the national tariff they retain the difference, but if their costs are higher than the tariff the hospital will be forced to cut costs, do more operations to generate additional income, or terminate the service. The system is designed to make money follow patients and to spur competition between hospitals. A Market Forces Factor, consisting of staff, buildings and land indices, is used to adjust the national tariff to give the local price for each Trust.

Payment by Results was designed to improve efficiency and value for money, facilitate choice and plurality, and increase contestability, and to 'get the price "right" for services which reflects true costs and incentivises patient care'. However, it 'creates an unprecedented level of financial risk for primary care trusts (PCTs) and trusts and greater potential for financial instability across the system as a whole' (Audit Commission, 2005). The Audit Commission found that the sample of organisations in their study had spent £100,000 each, equivalent to £50m nationally, yet found 'little evidence at the system level that the new incentives have generated the positive behaviours intended' (ibid). They concluded that a mechanism needed to be in place when a service or a trust becomes 'unviable' yet is vital for emergency patients and local access to quality care.

Practice-Based Commissioning: GP practices have the right to hold an indicative budget from the Primary Care Trust so that they can directly commission services. A move from a historical to a weighted capitation based budget is agreed locally.

Child Care Vouchers: The child care voucher market is expanding – employers commission a child care voucher company to provide vouchers for employees, either as a 'salary sacrifice' of up to £50 per week (free of tax and National Insurance contributions) or on top of the employee's salary. The vouchers can then be used by the employee to pay for registered or approved child care from any provider.

Child Trust Fund vouchers: Each child born in the UK after 1 September 2002 receives a £250 voucher to be invested in a savings, stakeholder or shares Child Trust Fund, operated by over 70 financial institutions. Families on low incomes receive a £500 voucher. They are another example of the shift towards an asset-based welfare state. The idea is that funds are topped up by family and friends, up to a maximum of £1,200 per annum. Funds are exempt from income and capital gains tax. Money cannot be accessed until a child is 18 when, if regular payments have been made into the Fund, enough should have accumulated to contribute towards university fees!

Decent Homes limited options appraisal: Local authorities are required to carry out an options appraisal to assess how they are able to meet the Decent Homes Standard by 2010. The Government restricted the options for increased investment to large scale voluntary transfer (LSVT), the private finance initiative (PFI), and arms length management organisation (ALMO). It argued strongly that there was 'no fourth way' of an authority retaining its stock and gaining additional investment through prudential borrowing. The options appraisal was centrally fixed, with choice proscribed for tenants (despite surveys showing 75% of tenants wanting to remain council tenants) and for local authorities. In effect the government made a decision to terminate the council housing tenure (The Case for the 4th option for Council Housing, Centre for Public Services, 2004).

58 local authorities out of the 192 that were required to have their options appraisals approved by government by the end of July 2005 failed to do so. 17 councils had still to submit proposals and 41 were still awaiting approval. Of the 138 authorities which have had their plans approved, 63 chose to retain their stock, 23 set up an arms length management organisation, and 46 chose stock transfer (*Inside Housing*, 5 August 2005).

The government admitted that the 2010 Decent Homes target will be missed by 10% (*Inside Housing*, 23 September 2005).

Dictate from the centre, no local choice despite local capacity: Northumberland, Tyne and Wear Strategic Health Authority (NTWSHA) demonstrated that the 18 week waiting time target for 2008 'could be achieved through NHS planned capital schemes and increased efficiency, without increasing Independent Sector provision', but the Department of Health reviewed the plan, acknowledged the Authority's conclusions, but 'outlined the requirement for NTWSHA to commit to its share of the phase 2 Independent Sector procurement for electives and diagnostic work' (Director of Nursing and Service Improvement, Report to NTWSHA Board, May 2005). The Authority did not need to use the private sector for elective surgery, but was told by the Department of Health that it had no choice.

Housing Corporation opens social housing grant to private developers: Social housing grant to build and refurbish affordable homes, previously restricted to non-profit housing associations, is now open to competition from private developers. Four private developers (Bellway, Bovis, First Base and Persimmon) and 13 housing associations were successful in a 2005 pilot project, but only £140m of the £200m was allocated because of poor quality bids. The Housing Corporation announced that the full £3.3bn programme for 2006-08 will be open to private sector bidding before it had evaluated the pilot. Many private sector bids were rejected because they attempted to use the pilot to obtain extra funding for schemes already approved or being subsidised through planning agreements! Despite failing to allocate all the pilot money, the Housing Corporation claimed that '... that there is a real market for private sector involvement in the delivery of new affordable homes' (Housing Corporation press release 99/05).

Some housing associations have formed consortia with private builders, others have established new development companies – 'It is becoming increasingly difficult for many in the outside world to distinguish between a housing association and a developer' (*Inside Housing*, 9 September 2005). In addition to joining forces with private developers and building for sale, housing associations are also diversifying into community care and regeneration, investing in NHS Local Improvement Finance Trust projects, and sponsoring academies in a period of merger mania. This is further proof of the dangers of hiving off services and assets to unaccountable third sector organisations.

Economic development: Many local authorities set up economic development companies as vehicles to attract inward investment, promote the local economy, and undertake specific projects. Government funding regimes often require or encourage provision by the private or voluntary sectors.

Creating market mechanisms
● Increasing choice – encouraging competition between schools and hospitals – this also creates the conditions for a market to operate.
● Secondary markets established in the refinancing of privately funded projects to take advantage of risk reduction – state colludes by agreeing profit-sharing arrangements to appease market.
● Brokerages promoted for school support services, which act as a purchasing agency enabling schools to procure goods and services.
● Councils told to 'encourage a mixed range of suppliers to help stimulate a varied and competitive market place' (Office of the Deputy Prime Minister, 2003).
● Setting regulations for the market to control prices, to try to prevent 'cherry picking' or 'cream skimming', and 'parking' difficult clients, and reducing 'red tape' for private firms.

● Regulatory Impact Assessments carried out for all policy changes to minimise obligations on private firms.

Examples
Child care, nursery and after school provision: The UK children's day nursery market was worth £3.2 billion in 2004. About 145 major providers (three or more nurseries) account for 14.5% of total UK places. About 20 companies dominate the private sector's 9% share of the market. Nord Anglia is the leading company with 102 nurseries, but they account for only 1.6% of the market (Children's Nurseries 2005. Laing & Buisson, 2005).

Secondary market in private finance initiative/public private partnership refinancing: Once an infrastructure project is built and operational, the project risks (such as delays in construction and site difficulties) are no longer relevant. Completion of the riskiest phase of the project successfully means that the investment market considers that the project will have increased in value and refinancing in effect enables the private sector to expropriate this value. Financial institutions are prepared to refinance projects offering better terms to reflect the lower risks (National Audit Office, 2002).

The sheer scale of investment is requiring construction companies to recycle or sell some of their equity or reschedule debt in private finance initiative projects in order to bid for new projects.

Several dedicated secondary market investments funds (for example Barclays/Soc Gen and Innisfree/M&G) have been set up to acquire private finance initiative equity. These funds will normally purchase the entire equity in a project and are planning to build a portfolio of private finance initiative projects. In other words, ownership of prisons, schools and hospitals will transfer from construction company-led consortia to financial investment institutions. This, in turn, is creating new markets for companies undertaking due diligence during the refinancing process and in managing groups of special purpose vehicle companies established for each private finance initiative project (Hazell, 2005).

A voluntary code was introduced in 2002, in which the private sector agreed to provide the public sector with 30% of any refinancing gain. However, this was not contractually binding. Refinancing of later private finance initiative projects is on a 50%/50% basis and is an integral part of HM Treasury's 'Standardisation of Private Finance Initiative Contracts' which requires the contractor to obtain an authority's consent to refinance a project (HM Treasury, 2005).

Refinancing 12 private finance initiative projects between 1999-2005 resulted in £142.6m gain for private finance initiative consortia, compared to £27.3m for the public sector (National Audit Office 2000, 2002, 2004, and 2005). Refinancing enables the private sector to increase the profitability of the private finance initiative over and above the average 15% – 20% return which is built into projects before refinancing. Laing sold a 50% stake in UK Highways (operates a section of M40) in October 2004 for £26.3m, making a 33% profit.

Schools Brokerage Services: A brokerage replaces schools purchasing services from the local education authority and local authority by providing access to a range of services and choice of quality assessed providers. A brokerage uses framework contracts to deliver each service or group of services with a number of suppliers. Schools 'exercise choice' without the need to undertake another formal tendering process. The brokerage operates as shop window for schools to buy goods and services as, for example, done by Essex County Council.

Conservative government's Deregulation and Contracting Out Act 1994 provisions copied into Labour's Regulatory Reform Act 2001: The government is able to make Orders to amend or repeal provisions in primary legislation which are considered to impose a burden on business or others. A PricewaterhouseCoopers study on the market for children's services showed that following a contracting out order under section 70 of the 1994 Act, 'local authorities have been able to contract out some core functions of their education services. This has resulted in the outsourcing to private providers of some education functions in a few local authorities. The Connexions and School Improvement markets are two examples where legal barriers have been removed and there has been the deliberate introduction of competition' (Department for Education and Skills, 2004).

Market driven planning system: The Barker Report concluded that high house price inflation could be reduced by increasing the supply of land for housing development (HM Treasury 2004) – a view challenged by many housing and planning bodies (*Inside Housing* 9 and 16 September 2005, *Building* 9 September 2005). The government has accepted the Barker recommendations, and plans to remove local authorities' power to decide when to release land and to order mandatory release of land when the price of homes relative to income in an area is above a certain level. This will trigger more house-building in popular areas and institutionalise 'managed reduction' in other areas, making regeneration and renewal more difficult. Until now the planning system has sought to balance market pressures with local planning objectives, public interest, sustainable development, and demographic change. Barker also accepted the trickle down thesis that a massive expansion of owner occupation will ultimately benefit the homeless – an idea without evidence to support it, which has plagued housing policy for years (see page 99 for dramatic rise in waiting lists and homelessness).

The government response to the Barker Review also proposed 'allowing local authorities with arms length management organisations the flexibility to use their own resources (including land) to build and own homes; exploring innovative ways in which excellent local authorities with good housing services could build new homes for rent; increasing the effectiveness of the housing private finance initiative programme, where Government is exploring the possibility of developing some form of partnership model to build new homes, which could speed up procurement and reduce its costs; and encouraging local authorities undertaking private finance initiative procurements to consider, with the private sector, the opportunities for increased new build for sale or shared ownership, which would be facilitated by the private finance initiative credits. This helps maximise income to the private finance initiative project, helping to reduce the cost to the public sector' (HM Treasury and Office of the Deputy Prime Minister, 2005). The government is also undertaking a cross cutting review 'to effectively coordinate the strategic delivery of infrastructure investment across departments' in the preparation of the 2007 Comprehensive Spending Review (ibid). Further marketisation and privatisation proposals are inevitable.

Local authorities are being urged to outsource planning services and 'free up council staff to work on more contentious and strategic issues' (Audit Commission, 2006). The Commission advocates a mixed economy approach with the private sector more widely used for core planning functions despite finding few examples of good practice. The Audit Commission makes the ridiculous claim that the government has 'recast planning as a strategic, proactive force' which is 'a shift from planning's previously narrow, regulatory function' (ibid).

Regeneration: The combined effects of the government's drive to increase homeownership, extend privately financed development through PFI, REITS, and mixed communities ('proactive de-concentration of deprivation'), award social housing grant to developers and transfer responsibility to arms length companies, further privatise the regeneration process.

New Growth Points Initiative: A new 'planning by competition' initiative has been launched with up to £40m capital funding for a first round of site infrastructure projects to help new growth points overcome local infrastructure problems. 'Local partners' in the South East, East, South West, East and West Midlands can apply. The North is excluded. The guidance refers only to 'local partners' and never mentions local government (Office of the Deputy Prime Minister, 2005). Proposals must have at least 20% housing growth above the pre-Sustainable Communities Plan baseline with overall housing growth of at least 500 homes per annum.

Housing Market Renewal Pathfinders: Nine projects have been established in the Midlands and North to deal with housing market failure resulting in low demand and abandonment. Projects include demolition, refurbishment and new housing using public/private investment and acquisition of land. Each area has a renewal team and consultancy budget funded by the Office of the Deputy Prime Minister.

Rail privatisation: The Conservative government's privatisation of British Rail in 1996 created a fragmented, publicly subsidised network with a worse performance record. The franchises and competitive regime has been heavily subsidized; train operators received £1.8bn in 2003/04 alone, accounting for about 20% of their income (Shaoul, 2005). Some £890m has been taken out of the rail industry in dividends to shareholders. Fares have risen faster than the rate of inflation whilst wages have fallen behind average earnings. In 1993/94, British Rail InterCity and regional services ran 90.6% and 90.3% to time respectively. In the year ending 31 March 2005, long distance and regional services ran only 79.1% and 82.7% to time respectively (ibid).

In December 2005, European Union Transport Ministers agreed to further liberalisation of railways, basically applying the British model across Europe in the implementation of Directive 91/440/EEC. This will force a vertical split between trains and track ('wheels and steel') with operational autonomy for railway operators, open access for cross border undertakings, and track access charges.

Marketised vocational education and training – lessons from Australia: Some 230 state-run institutes operating from a 1,000 locations previously delivered technical and further education in Australia. By the mid-1990s this had been replaced by a competitive market with private providers given access to government recognition and funding. A national evaluation of the marketised system 'identified several benefits and costs of market-based competition ... On balance, the weight of available evidence suggests that, currently, negative rather than positive outcomes predominate. Outcomes appear to be positive in relation to choice and diversity, responsiveness (to medium/large enterprises and fee-paying clients), flexibility, and innovation. Outcomes appear to be generally negative in relation to efficiency (due largely to high transaction costs and complexity), responsiveness (to small enterprises, local/surrounding communities, and government-subsidised students), quality, and access and equity' (National Centre for Vocational Education Research, 2006).

Regulators appointed to manage liberalisation
● The Postal Services Commission (Postcomm) was established to marketise the postal service and Monitor was established to regulate Foundation Hospitals.

Examples
Establishing 'Regulators' who then 'open up markets': Labour's Postal Services Act 2000 included establishment of a regulator, Postcomm, and a regulatory framework that 'facilitates a competitive and innovative postal market.' This followed the 1997 European Union Postal Services Directive aimed at the liberalisation of Europe's state-run postal services. But Royal Mail lost its 350-year monopoly over the delivery of letters in January 2006, well ahead of other European countries (Germany and Holland in 2007 and the rest in 2009). Since March 2001, Postcomm has issued 14 long-term licences to private postal companies such as TNT, DHL (Deutsche Post) and UK Mail (Business Post). Royal Mail lost an estimated 1.5% market share in the first six months of 2005/06 compared with only 0.3% in the entire year in 2003/04 (*Financial Times*, 29 December 2005).

Postcomm is financed (£10m annual budget with 53 staff) by Royal Mail licence fees. Six of the seven 'independent' commissioners are from the private sector. It also controls Royal Mail's prices.

Postcomm issued proposals to reduce barriers to entry to the market in March 2005. The economic logic of marketisers is worth setting out.

1. Royal Mail has economies of scale because its network reaches all residential and commercial addresses in the UK. It also has a national network of post boxes. But a universal service turns from being an

advantage to a 'barrier to entry' in the market. So Postcomm has 'facilitated downstream access' to Royal Mail's network and delivery network for private postal companies to enable 'competition in marketing, collection, sorting and trunking activities'.

2. Royal Mail has VAT exempt status, which creates a 'distortion' in the market because private postal companies' services to non-VAT recovering customers are at a disadvantage (although this is estimated to be a 13% price advantage because Royal Mail cannot reclaim VAT on supplies). Another barrier to entry! So there must be, to use a hackneyed phrase, a level playing field. Postcomm's solution is a uniform rate of 5% VAT for all postal operators.

3. Postcomm believes that Royal Mail will use its dominant position to indulge in 'anti-competitive behaviour' and promises swift response to complaints of this activity.

4. Postcomm believes that customers are 'not generally well informed about the liberalisation of the market' so plan a series of events to raise awareness (Tackling Barriers to Entry in Postal Services, Postcomm, March 2005).

Thus, a regulatory agency, supposedly 'the guardian of the universal service'. spends its resources creating the conditions and regulations to maximise private sector involvement in the postal service, which will ultimately undermine the universal service.

Royal Mail management believe that 'competitors will actually set up delivery forces, for instance, in major city centres, which is where there is a lot of money to be made, and simply put the rest of the mail, the more unprofitable mail, into the Royal Mail for it to deliver, and that is what we call "cream skimming" (House of Commons Trade and Industry Committee, 2005). Royal Mail and the Communication Workers Union also believe that competitors will be free to 'cherry pick' the profitable services which could undermine Royal Mail's ability to provide a universal service. Access arrangements also threaten Royal Mail in which private companies collect and sort mail for corporate clients and Royal Mail deliver 'the final mile' for a fixed fee.

Centralisation of inspection: The government is planning to centralise eleven inspectorates into four super-inspectorates. The Audit Commission and the Benefit Fraud Inspectorate will become the inspectorate of local services. The Healthcare Commission will take over adult care from the Commission for Social Care Inspectorate with OFSTED taking over responsibility for inspecting children's services. It will also take over the Children and Family Court Advisory and Support Services and the Adult Learning Inspectorate. A fourth inspectorate will cover justice and community safety.

The Healthcare Commission is planning to refocus its inspection regime with fewer inspections targeted on the effectiveness of commissioners of services (*Health Service Journal*, 29 September 2005). So just when the private sector takes over an even larger slice of health and social care provision, the inspection regime will have a 'lighter touch' with spot checks on providers 'for consumer protection purposes' (ibid). Inspection regimes will target how well the public sector 'commissions' services, which will include how they manage contracts. So the blame culture will continue, leaving service users and staff sandwiched between contractual and legal disputes between commissioners and providers.

Changing operational priorities
● Efficiency campaign following Gershon Review to speed up the number and range of services going through procurement process, increasing outsourcing and thus expanding marketisation.
● Boundaries between public and private sector provision and organisational responsibilities are eroded thus diluting matters of public interest and the public domain. Public bodies required to be responsible for private and public sector provision.
● Business units and arms length companies search for 'competitive edge' (an apparent advantage over other providers) and niche markets (offering specific service not supplied by other competitors) and select profit maximising services.
● Switching local/regional supply chains to national/global sourcing to maximise efficiency and economies of scale.
● Widening the range of services, including core functions, in contracts.
● Public sector intellectual capital is transferred at little or no cost to the private sector via consultants, framework agreements, partnerships and joint ventures.
● Spare capacity created to facilitate operation of the market.
● Closing facilities and withdrawing from service provision.
● Public sector organisations are encouraged to adopt the private sector's model of 'corporate citizen' and corporate social responsibility as the means of demonstrating their social and environmental credentials.
● Concordats between state and private sector to establish market mechanisms, for example between the NHS and private health firms,

and between local authorities and small and medium sized enterprises for procurement.

● Brokering changes in social relations between the state, citizens, trade unions, private contractors and voluntary bodies, from public service principles to market mechanisms.

Examples

Remit of the Housing Corporation changed to include private sector: The Housing Corporation finances, regulates and facilitates the performance of Britain's 2,000 housing associations. The aims and objectives of the Corporation were changed in April 2005 and now refer to the payment of grants for new stock and refurbishment of existing stock, the provision of decent homes, effective housing services and sustainable communities by registered social landlords *and* non-registered social landlords, ie the private sector (Office of Deputy Prime Minister/Housing Corporation, 2005).

Regional Centres of Excellence (RCE) for procurement and efficiency: Established to help mainstream procurement in local government but their remit was extended to efficiency following the Gershon Report in 2004. The regional centres of excellence will provide support and 'change agents' from other government agencies, analyse local authority procurement performance, and encourage shared working across authorities including private and voluntary sector involvement. The Department for Education and Skill's Centre for Procurement Performance has a similar role in education.

Closure of residential homes: Places in local authority care homes declined dramatically from 85,000 in 1994 to only 44,200 a decade later. Many local authorities sold their residential homes to the private and voluntary sector. Others closed homes or turned them into resource centres. Local authorities such as Rochdale, Newcastle and Barnet have no council-run residential homes for the elderly.

Aggressive 'thrive to survive' tactics by hospitals and schools: 'A rapid and brutal shake-out of the poorest performers' was advocated by Martin Hensher, an NHS Confederation policy manager advising the government on the failure regime under choice and payment by results. 'If there were going to be major changes to the sector which were needed by the market, we would rather it was done quicker', he added ('Brutal approach to market', *Health Service Journal*, 23 June 2005).

Cost of closures: Hospitals and schools that fail to attract sufficient patients and pupils in the market regime will be allowed to close. 'I am not envisaging rapid, wholesale closure of facilities' (Hewitt warns that failing hospitals will be closed, *Financial Times*, 14 May 2005). So closures are planned.

Privatisation of assets and services

● Privatisation creates markets by transferring ownership and responsibility to the private sector, which then sources goods and services from other private companies.
● Encouraging the sales of assets by government departments, local authorities, NHS trusts and other public bodies, for example the sale of council and housing association homes, to 'widen the market', but in reality embedding an asset-based welfare state, in which benefits are determined by access to assets rather than as a citizen's right.

Examples
Academy schools

Sponsors provide 10% of the capital costs with a £2m cap or £1.5m for refurbished schools. The government provides the balance of between £20m – £30m. Academies are privately run, the Local Education Authority has no direct control in running the school. Sponsors employ their own staff (except where there is a predecessor school and Transfer of Undertakings (Protection of Employment) Regulations 1981 (TUPE) applies. They also appoint the majority of governors. 'Issues of ethos, specialism and uniform are entirely for you' plus 'the vast majority of the detail (curriculum) will be for you' states the Academies Sponsors Prospectus (Department for Education and Skills, 2005).

By autumn 2005, some 27 academies were opened with 30 more in the pipeline. Almost half of the new academies are sponsored by religious groups, others include the chairmen of financial services companies, stockbrokers, outsourcing company Capita, a recruitment agency, Lord Harris (three) the ex-carpet chain owner, and Lord Laidlaw who bankrolls the Scottish Tories. Corporate sponsors include the private finance initiative contractor Amey plc, Pfizer, the pharmaceutical company, and Dixons, the electronics retailer. To the delight of the Department for Education and Skills, the National Housing Federation and stock transfer consultants Trial HCH, New Charter Housing Trust became the first housing association sponsor with a new secondary school in Greater Manchester (*Inside Housing*, 2005).

Of the 13 academies which replaced schools that were in special measures or had serious weaknesses, all the 'failing' schools were improving educational standards and none were in special measures when they were closed (*Guardian*, 8 October 2005). OFSTED reports on schools in Middlesbrough, Bradford and Doncaster referred to 'rapidly improving', 'very effective school', and 'an improving and increasingly effective school, which cares well for its pupils' respectively.

The academies' claim 'to bring new life into the local community' is fraudulent because they are caught in a VAT trap. The Treasury waived VAT on the construction costs under European VAT regulations, but this is conditional on 90% of the usage being for 'relevant charitable purposes'. Thus academies must limit after school use to less than an hour per day and not at all during holidays or face a VAT bill for 17.5% of the capital cost of the school. Martin Coles, head of the City of London Academy in Bermondsey, South London, stated: 'We have this £27m building and the public can't get in. It's a joke' (*Times*, 3 October 2005).

Governance and accountability, business sponsorship, performance, admissions/selection, inequalities, funding, curriculum, workforce and trade union recognition are some of the key issues with respect to academies. The most recent annual review of academy performance showed that of 11 which were open in 2004, six improved their GCSE performance and five did not (Department for Education and Skills, 2005). '… The composition of governing bodies in Academies is that they were co-opted from business and/or the personal circumstance of the sponsors' (ibid). The House of Commons Education and Skills Committee concluded 'Despite the Government's attachment to evidence-based policy, expensive schemes are rolled out before being adequately tested and evaluated compared to other less expensive alternatives' (House of Commons, 2005). A regularly updated academies briefing is available from the NUT web site (www.teachers.org.uk). Academies have yet to prove that they can improve educational performance at a faster rate than other initiatives with the same resources starting from similar a low base.

Sale and lease-back of government offices
The New Labour government, keen to establish a market in the sale and lease-back of government buildings, announced a £3.6 billion private finance initiative deal with Mapeley Group in March 2001. It included 700 buildings of the Inland Revenue, HM Customs and

Excise, and the Valuation Office Agency in the Strategic Transfer of the Estate to the Private Sector (STEPS) project. It was similar to an earlier private finance initiative project by the Department of Work and Pensions for the Newcastle Estate. Under sale and lease-back, the state sells buildings that are maintained by private sector property management companies for 21 years, who then find other tenants/uses.

Mapeley immediately transferred the freehold and long-lease properties to Bermuda. Mapeley is owned by Fortress Investment Group, USA, Soros Real Estate, Netherlands and Delancy East Ltd, UK, but now based offshore in Bermuda. The Strategic Transfer of the Estate to the Private Sector is expected to save £344m over the 20-year contract period. However, Mapeley estimated that it would have had to increase its bid price by £55m to bring the STEPS properties onshore: in other words, the Inland Revenue lost £55m income because of the deal. But the shareholders of Mapeley are non-UK resident and do not have to pay UK capital gains if they sell their shareholdings – this is a potential additional loss of income for Inland Revenue. Inland Revenue knew about the offshore plan during preferred bidder negotiations, but HM Customs and Excise were not informed until after the contract was signed!

Seven months into the contract, Mapeley demanded more money based on errors in pricing its bid and the level of contract variations, and claimed an annual shortfall of £27m. Mapeley's bid was some £500m lower than two other bids. The Departments refused to pay and the firm's shareholders injected additional finance. Four years into the contract the performance management system had still not been agreed. By April 2004 the Departments had spent an additional £13m on consultants for the STEPS project.

Committee of Public Accounts, Wednesday 27 October 2004, Oral Evidence: Edward Leigh, chair of the Committee introducing the session: 'Mr Varney, does it not give the Inland Revenue any sense of shame that they are now known as a well known tax avoider!' David Varney, Executive chairperson, Inland Revenue/Customs and Excise: 'I do not think they are known as a well known tax avoider' (House of Commons, 2005).

Yet the National Audit Office made no comment on the offshore aspects of the deal except that the £55m was 'not material'. However, they did recognise that the STEPS business model 'has a high degree of fixed costs and is therefore very sensitive to any future shortfalls in forecast income'. Civil servants appearing before the Committee of Public Accounts could not give any assurances on whether the £344m savings will be achieved or not. Despite all the pitfalls with this project, the National Audit Office claimed that 'STEPS had demonstrated a number of benefits both for departments and for bidders, for example, reduced costs and a more attractive portfolio of properties' (National Audit Office, 2004). The evidence shows only that it may have reduced costs in the first four years of a twenty-year contract. The only certainty is that the private sector gets an 'attractive portfolio of properties' from such deals.

Large scale stock transfers create new markets: Over 130 council housing stock transfers (over 1m homes with 76.5% of transfers having taken place under a Labour government) to housing associations created new markets in financing and arranging private finance, and for housing consultancies in options appraisals and so-called tenants' friend consultants. It also led to a market developing in firms of tenants' participation advisers who were employed by local authorities to provide 'independent advice' to tenants in the run-up to transfer ballots and option appraisals in the Decent Homes initiative.

Right to Buy continues: The sale of council homes increased 50% between 1997/98 and 2003/04. Total UK sales of 95,607 homes in 2004/05 was over five times the number of new homes completed by housing associations with local authorities contributing a mere 207 new homes. The number of households on housing waiting lists has increased 52% since 1997, and homelessness has more than doubled from 43,520 in the second quarter of 1997 to 100,970 in the same quarter in 2005 (Office of the Deputy Prime Minister 2005 and Hansard, Parliamentary Answer, 17 October 2005).

Extending the sale of council housing and housing association dwellings: The new HomeBuy scheme aims to assist 100,000 households to purchase their home by 2010. Social HomeBuy enables council and housing association tenants to buy a share in their current home at a discount, starting with a minimum 25% stake and increasing in 10% tranches to full ownership. It will cost the taxpayer £30m for every 5,000 dwellings sold. New Build HomeBuy enables people to buy a share in a newly built property, and Open Market HomeBuy allows people to buy a property on the open market.

New Real Estate Investment Trusts (REITs): Although new in Britain, real estate property trusts already exist in several other European Union countries. real estate property trusts will invest in commercial and residential property, and pay no corporation tax, in return for distributing 95% of net profits to investors. Three-quarters of the income of a real estate property trust must come from property rents. They can be included in pension schemes, individual savings accounts (ISAs), personal equity plans (PEPs) and child trust funds (CFTs). Most property companies are expected to convert to real estate property trusts, although no shareholder will be able to own more than 10% of any trust. Some housing associations are considering establishing real estate property trusts.

Restructuring democratic accountability and user involvement

The marketisation process relies heavily on changing the social, economic and political expectations and aspirations of existing and potential users. The government is trying to achieve choice via competition in the marketplace – service users are treated as, and they must identify themselves as, individual consumers, who make decisions primarily in their own self-interest. This process also leads to the transfer of more services from direct democratic accountability to the private sector or arms length companies. The concept of collective provision through area based or social groups is marginalised. Thus 'consumers' are encouraged to relate to the organisation individually, rather than collectively, through user and community organisations.

Treating users as individual consumers and purchasers
● Citizens and users are treated as individual consumers rather than as service users with collective interests and rights.
● Choice is promoted via the right to select any school or hospital, supposedly based on performance, with money following pupils and patients.
● Ideology of mixed economy, private sector and business efficiency, choice and 'neutrality' on who provides services promoted in media.
● Weaken universal and redistributive public service provision, which is replaced by provision through market forces.
● Financial autonomy is accompanied by new user rights to complain and demand a new facility or service provider. This will be engineered, as with the private finance initiative in schools and hospitals, so that there is no alternative to the private sector. It is also intended to create divisions and sectional interests in communities so

that communities are left with no choice.

● Direct payments systems, vouchers, and individual budgets provide public money to individuals who then choose a service provider.

● Increased user charges and replacing students grants with loans are another form of replacing public with private finance.

● Market research techniques used to replace or reduce channels for user participation and involvement in public policy making.

Examples

Direct payments in lieu of services: First introduced in 1997 for working age adults, direct payments have been extended to older people and to parents of disabled children and carers. The Green Paper, *Independence, Well-Being and Choice*, proposes to extend direct payments to young disabled people, people with dementia, and people with profound learning disabilities. The government proposes the use of 'agents' for those without the capacity to consent or unable to manage in order to increase the use of direct payments – 12,585 individuals were in receipt of direct payments in 2003 compared to 1.68m adults using community care services (Department of Health, 2005).

Currently, people using direct payments can buy services from any provider except a local authority! The government intends to pilot 'individual budgets', which would be held by the local authority, and people could choose which services they want, and receive support in the form of a direct payment or the provision of services. 'The ability of people to 'buy' elements of their care or support package will stimulate the social care market to provide the services people actually want, and help shift resources away from services which do not meet needs and expectations' (Department of Health, 2005).

Community care charges: Most local authorities now impose charges for home care services based on age, income and savings.

Individual Learning Accounts: In July 2000 Capita Group PLC won a contract to operate the Individual Learning Account (ILA) scheme under which everyone aged 19 or over had a right to an Account entitling them up to chose how they spent up £200 on training. Between its September 2000 launch and its closure on 21 November 2001 there were 2.5m accounts logged on to Capita's computer system. The scheme was closed because there were suspicions that abuse of the scheme had become so endemic that they could not be eradicated without killing the scheme itself (House of Commons, 2002). The scheme cost £268.8m with an overspend of £69.9m. Capita received nearly 8,500 complaints by the end of October 2002. Its security was later described as pitiful, and vetting procedures for learning providers as 'shocking', in evidence to the Select Committee (ibid). The level of abuse and fraud was estimated to run into millions and, by August 2002, 560 learning providers were under investigation by the Department's compliance unit, and 99 had been transferred to the police (National Audit Office, 2002).

Child care vouchers: The first £50 a week supplied via childcare vouchers is exempt from tax and national insurance. Vouchers can be used to pay any form of registered or approved childcare. Employers normally provide vouchers via a childcare voucher company. The new benefit had resulted in a large increase in the number of voucher schemes. There are several childcare voucher companies – the process of consolidation has already begun. Sodexho Pass acquired Family Matters in 2005.

The children's day nursery market was worth £3.2bn in 2004 (Laing & Buisson, 2005). Parents spent an estimated £2.7bn (84%), employers spent 6.5%, and central government spent £240m on subsidies. The average full-time fee was £134 per week in early 2005. The market is very fragmented with 145 providers operating 3 or more nurseries but accounting for just 14.5% of places (ibid).

Student grants abolished and tuition fees introduced in England and Wales: The system of tax-financed student support was abolished in 1998 alongside the introduction of tuition fees. From 2006, the flat fee is replaced by a variable fee of up to £3,000 per annum. Students loans were extended so that students can take an additional loan to cover tuition fees, alongside increased loans for living costs. Graduates will have to repay 9% of earnings above £15,000. There are no tuition fees in Scotland.

Markets rely on access to information: A national study of care homes for elderly people found that there was a lack of awareness among older people and their representatives about sources of information, confusion about what advice and support authorities should be providing, a lack of transparency about care homes and terms and conditions for living in a care home (Office of Fair Trading, 2005).

Dubious surveys and opinion polls: Market survey and polling companies are jumping on the bandwagon with telephone surveys of 'patient preferences' for Strategic Health Authorities and private healthcare companies. These are used to 'justify' patient choice by playing on patient fears and simplistic questions devoid of knowledge about private health companies, real options and healthcare information (*Health Service Journal*, 21 July 2005).

Transferring responsibility to quangos and third sector organisations
● Transfer to arms length companies and trusts, setting up new organisations, partnership boards, turning schools and hospitals into stand alone businesses (the foundation model), and encouraging expansion of social enterprises to deliver public services.
● Transfer of services to arms length companies, trusts and quasi-private/public bodies to provide services as alternative to direct public provision – arms length management organisations, foundation hospitals and schools, leisure trusts, housing associations, most of which outsource services. One of the aims is to create autonomous business units which will compete against each other to create choice (a partial system in reality), but also further fragments and weakens direct public provision.

Examples
Urban Development Corporations (UDCs): Urban Development Corporations (UDCs) have been established in the growth areas in the south-east to takeover responsibility for coordinating development. For example, in Thurrock in the Thames Gateway, the Urban Development Corporation boundary is coterminous with the local authority boundary and the Corporation has recently taken over strategic planning powers from the local authority. Thurrock outsourced 750 staff in a 15-year strategic partnership covering financial services, information and communication technology, human resources, facilities and property management, highways and transportation services to Vertex and United Utilities in April 2005. The combination of these two developments represents a significant loss of direct control for the local authority. West Northamptonshire Development Corporation is set to take control of all new development applications in Northampton, despite original resistance from the council.
Urban Regeneration Companies (URCs): Since 2000, twenty-two urban regeneration companies have taken over responsibility for major regeneration areas. Each urban regeneration company is supported by the Regional Development Agency, English Partnerships, and the local authority, and has local business and community representation on the board. To date some £900m of public investment has been matched equally by the private sector. However, the chief executive of

English Partnerships has called for urban regeneration companies to 'sweat the assets' and to achieve a 20/80 public/private share of investment (English Partnerships Press Release, 8 September 2005).

Arms length housing management companies: Council housing, leisure and social care provision has been transferred to arms length companies or trusts in many local authorities. Boards of directors usually include one-third business/independent members. Companies and trusts can continue to use council services for a limited period before procuring and contracting their own goods and services. 40 arms length management organisations, 60 leisure trusts, 21 Urban Regeneration Companies and potentially hundreds of Building Schools for the Future and Foundation schools will significantly expand private markets. The Audit Commission is putting pressure on arms length management organisations to review service level agreements with local authorities, partly to demonstrate they are 'truly arms length' and to ensure procurement decisions are in the best interest of tenants, not the council ('ALMOs look to axe council contracts', *Inside Housing*, 13 May 2005). Thus, community well-being benefits in procurement are replaced by narrow 'client' financial interests. Some arms length management organisations are bidding to run services in other ALMOs – Brent and Kensington and Chelsea submitted a joint bid to run housing services in Westminster's arms length management organisation (*Inside Housing*, 30 September 2005).

Arms length management organisations are also concerned that they are 'running a shrinking business' as a result of right-to-buy sales reducing the housing stock. This is contributing to debates about potential mergers, and demands for greater financial freedom to build new homes.

Some policies such as arms length management organisations and academies are claimed to be a 'success' when, in fact, higher levels of performance and satisfaction are a result of increased public investment, and there is no evidence that the new organisational models are the source of the improvements. Tenant satisfaction in 43 arms length management organisations increased to an average 77% in 2004/5, raising them marginally above housing association performance (Office of Deputy Prime Minister survey found 75%/65% housing association/council housing satisfaction levels) (*HouseMark*, 2005). However, this is hardly surprising since arms length management organisations are in the process of a multi-million pound improvement programme renewing kitchens, bathrooms, windows and so on. 'If you are improving a lot of people's houses then unless you are making a right mess of it they should be happier' concluded Andy Selman, company secretary of Kirklees Neighbourhood Housing (*Inside Housing*, 30 September 2005).

Stock Transfer Registered Social Landlords (RSLs): Sale of council housing stock by 135 local authorities (1.5m homes so far) to housing associations under the Large Scale Voluntary Transfer programme.

Leisure Trusts: Over 60 local authorities have transferred leisure services to Trusts, which are similar to arms length companies with Boards consisting of a third council, community and business representatives. Staff transferred to the Trust, which receives an annual operating grant from the council. Some Trusts, for example Greenwich and South Oxfordshire, have won contracts to operate leisure services in other local authorities.

Joint Venture Companies or Partnership Boards in Strategic Service-Delivery Partnerships: Boards normally consist of the council leader and senior cabinet members, the chief executive and a few service directors plus a director and senior managers from the private contractor, and report directly to the council's Executive (Middlesbrough, Bedfordshire). A few make minutes available but many are secretive.

Business Improvement Districts (BIDs): Business Improvement Districts are companies that take responsibility for managing services in a city or town centre, using provisions in the Local Government Act 2003. Local business interests can decide that they wish to improve city centre environments, form a Business Improvement District Board and hold a ballot of ratepayers, who will normally be required to pay an additional levy on the rates. This is likely to increase outsourcing, and erodes democratic accountability in towns and cities. There is no requirement that Business Improvement District Boards are electable (Office of the Deputy Prime Minister, 2003).

Foundation Hospitals: The increasing commercialisation of Foundation Hospitals is clearly evident in documents of the Foundation Trust Network (FTN), the alliance of Foundation Hospitals. The Network wants greater autonomy from government targets, a 'hands off' approach by the regulator (Monitor), removal of the cap on the number of private patients they can treat, to provide primary care services, and to be allowed to 'develop a reach beyond health'. Patients' needs can be met by adopting 'the Debenham model of providing branded boutiques' (sic) (Foundation Trust Network, 2005). The Network's conference 'Opportunities for Developing the Business', in September 2005, was based on the potential to 'act as entrepreneurs in the independent sector', 'developing new business models', and had sessions on 'building your brand', opportunities for equity investment, and set up a new network for directors with commercial development responsibilities (Foundation Trust Network, 2005).

NHS Trusts originally had to have a three star rating to apply for Foundation status, but this was relaxed in November 2005 (the government was forced to reduce a similar threshold for housing arms length management organisations).

Trusts and Foundation Schools: All secondary schools will be able to gain trust or foundation status by a vote of school governors and will be able to employ their own staff, own school buildings and playing fields, administer admissions, and enter 'partnerships' with other schools to provide for school improvement, provision for excluded pupils, and special educational needs.

'This is where the whole crackpot idea (of competing hospitals) breaks down. If a private sector organisation fails, it will go broke and close. But nobody is going to let Leeds General Infirmary shut. The minute you take away that sanction, most of the intellectual rigour of this so-called market collapses in a little heap.' (Frank Dobson, MP and former Secretary of State for Health, *Financial Times*, 4 July 2005).

Arms length and not-for-profit companies in health: East Elmbridge and Mid Surrey Primary Care Trust are considering establishing a not-for-profit company, Central Surrey Healthcare, with over 700 community nursing and therapy staff. It will provide specialist medical services directly to local commissioners such as the Trust itself, acute trusts, and the local education authority. The Trust recently received a zero star rating from the Healthcare Commission.

The Department of Health has 38 Arms Length Bodies (ALBs) employing 22,000 staff with a combined annual budget of £4.8bn. It plans to reduce the number to 20 by 2007/08, saving £0.5bn and cutting staff by 25%. They include the NHS Purchasing and Supply Agency (PASA), NHS Direct, NHS Logistics Authority (considering outsourcing the supply chain), NHS Business Services Authority, and NHS Blood and Transplant. Democratic accountability is a marginal concern in the review and reconfiguration proposals (Department of Health, 2004).

Local Public Service Boards: The government is considering the establishment of Public Service Boards, particularly 'where services are failing'. This would expand the role of local strategic partnerships (LSPs), and increase the scope for outsourcing (Office of the Deputy Prime Minister paper).

Other companies, trusts and boards: Many local authorities have set up economic development companies and arts trusts. Virtually all new government programmes require new organisational structures and boards, such as Housing Market Renewal Pathfinders and New Deal for Communities.

New quangos: Partnerships for Education and Partnerships for Health established by the Department for Education and Skills and the Department of Health respectively to implement private finance deals (see pages 77 to 82).

Setting up private sector organisations within public services
● New alternative privately controlled partnerships and arms length companies (the local education partnership) are created to take over responsibility for providing services (separated from the local authority, they are expected to marketise and privatise at a faster rate than the local education authority or local authority). Development of growth and major regeneration areas transferred to Urban Development Corporations and Urban Regeneration Companies with significant private sector involvement.
● Governance of organisations has to be brokered with business and 'independent' members of arms length companies and trusts.
● Arms length relationship imposes a hurdle or barrier and more complexity in access to elected members.

Examples
Local Education Partnerships in the Building Schools for the Future programme: The Local Education Partnership (LEP) is the delivery vehicle which builds and operates new and refurbished secondary schools, and potentially operates all local authority schools as part of the Building Schools for the Future programme. It is a joint venture company in which the private sector company normally has 80% of the shares, with the local authority and Partnership for Schools each having 10% of the share capital. The Partnership is managed by a Board of Directors with representation reflecting the shareholding. It prepares a business plan to deliver the Strategic Business Case. The

Partnership has a Strategic Partnering Agreement (SPA) under which it and the local authority agree to work together for 10 years (with an option for a further five). The agreement gives the Partnership exclusive rights to propose and deliver proposals to meet the Strategic Business Case. The new Local Education Partnership could ultimately replace local education authorities as it widens the range of services it delivers to schools, whilst the government recasts LEAs as commissioners (Department for Education and Skills, 2004 and Partnership for Schools, 2005). (See chapter 4 and above).

Embedding business interests and promoting liberalisation internationally

There are essentially three parts to this element of the marketisation process. Firstly, the state draws in business advisers and representatives on to task forces and project teams to develop public policy. Secondly, trade associations, representing contractors, constantly promote marketisation and competition through policy papers and 'think tanks', and complain vigorously about red tape, over-regulation, and any public body appearing to challenge the norm. Thirdly, private contractors reinforce the marketisation process by bidding for contracts, and building consortia increasing capacity through diversification, restructuring, takeovers and mergers to increase their ability to take on ever-larger and more complex contracts.

The European Union and World Trade Organisation proposals to liberalise services will greatly widen and embed markets and accelerate the outsourcing of services.

Business involvement in the public policy making process
● Promotion of competitive tendering, outsourcing and public private partnerships by trade associations, right wing think tanks, and contractors.
● Establishment of consultative mechanisms, membership of task forces, and project teams with central government and public bodies to promote business interests, minimise regulations and the threat of 'red tape'. Tolerating or encouraging 'revolving doors' – senior management move from public employment to private contractors. Often senior contract staff are poached by firms bidding for contracts. Government has facilitated a two-way exchange of senior staff between public and private sector, further eroding boundaries, in order to 'better understand the needs of business'.

● Business sector and wealthy individuals sponsoring academies
● Companies seconding senior staff to work on the planning and design of government programmes.

Examples
Strategic Service-Delivery Partnership Task Force to promote strategic partnerships: Five project teams were established for corporate services; transport and environment; health, social services and education; plus legal and technical and gateway teams. Forty-six of the fifty two members were from private contractors and management consultants, most of whom were bidding for or advising local authorities on strategic partnership projects.

Seconding senior managers to government departments: The head of local government services for Amey Infrastructure Services was seconded to be programme director for Building Schools for the Future at the Department for Education and Skills (*Project Finance Magazine*, May 2005).

Business invited to run Trust Schools: The Prime Minister regularly runs 'seminars' at Downing Street to which business is formally invited to express its interest in running public services. A recent example is one held in February 2006 for organisations interested in becoming school trusts. Microsoft, BT, Serco and management consultants KPMG were among the companies attending (*The Independent*, 10 February 2006). Cadbury Schweppes and other companies had further talks 'about helping to run state schools' with Ruth Kelly, Secretary of State for Education, in March 2006 (*Financial Times*, 7 March 2006).

NHS Partners Network: Tony Blair welcomed 11 private healthcare companies into the 'NHS family' at a Downing Street launch of the NHS Partners Network in February 2006. The 11 companies operate Independent Sector Treatment Centres (ISTCs) and include BUPA, Capio (Sweden), Interhealth Care Services (Canada), Nations Healthcare (US), Netcare (South Africa), BMI Healthcare and Mercury Health. This event 'coincided' with the publication of a report from the NHS Commercial Director glorifying the contribution of the private sector to NHS reform (DH, 2006).

Business and trade associations promote free trade in services
● Trade associations campaign for regulatory regimes in the interests of capital and seek to reduce 'red tape'. They also:

● Lobby government on public policies, spending programmes and procurement regulations.

● Promote further marketisation of public services through policy papers and company commissioned research studies by 'think tanks', which produce pro-privatisation findings.

● Monitor local authorities' and public bodies' responses to markets, and lodge complaints from their members whenever they perceive they are not operating in their interest. This 'evidence' is then used to argue for further deregulation, to build alliances and networks to promote marketisation and increased private provision.

● A wide range of international and national business organisations have constantly lobbied government and international agencies to advocate free trade in services and support for the European Union and World Trade Organisation liberalisation of services.

● Meetings are arranged between senior civil servants and directors of government agencies to meet with private sector companies to lay the ground for private sector participation in bidding for contracts.

Examples
Business organisations demanding service liberalisation: Business associations such as the European and British Chambers of Commerce, the Confederation of British Industry (CBI) and Institute of Directors, the Coalition of Service Industries, Transatlantic Business Dialogue and the World Economic Forum are just a few of the business interest organisations which have well-resourced campaigns demanding liberalisation and free trade. They also are represented at all levels in the European Union, the Organisation for Economic Cooperation and Development, the G8, G20, and World Trade Organisation meetings and negotiations.

Other trade groups such as the Business Services Association (BSA), representing the 20 major companies providing outsourced services in Britain, Europe and world-wide, and the Major Contractors Group (representing construction firms) campaign for more private finance initiative/public private partnership deals and support the government's outsourcing and choice agenda.

European Services Forum (ESF) and the US Coalition of Service Industries (CSI): These are two of many organisations (see Embedding Business Interests section) campaigning for the liberalisation of trade in services. European Services Forum members include 38 major companies and 36 service federations. They regularly meet with other business federations, attend trade negotiations, send trade missions, lobby governments and international organizations, and organise forums/networks of business interests, academics and government officials.

New trade groups of arms length companies and foundation hospitals: The National Association of Arms Length Management Organisations and the Foundation Trust Network were formed to represent the interests of ALMOs and Foundation hospitals. Both have lobbied the government for greater freedom and autonomy for arms length companies.

Business-led public sector reform: The Confederation of British Industry (CBI) and the New Local Government Network (NLGN) campaign for greater business involvement in the provision of public services and have a vested interest in extending marketisation. The CBI Public Services Strategy Board 'provides strategic direction for the CBI public service reform campaign', promoting business involvement in the delivery of public services. The Board is chaired by Rod Aldridge, chairperson of Capita Group, and has senior executives from Serco, Carillion, Accord, EDS, Fujitsu, Vertex, General Healthcare Group, KPMG, HBS Business Services and other private contractors.

The CBI Public Services Industry Forum organises briefings and events to bring together business leaders, civil servants, MPs and Ministers. There is also a CBI Education Providers Panel and the CBI study into private contracting in local education authorities (CBI, 2005,) which glorified outsourcing, and a Healthcare Panel 'to foster a positive dialogue between industry and the Department of Health.' The CBI wants to drive efficiency harder and further than the Gershon proposals, wants commercial directorates in government departments to manage public sector markets, and to outsource the administrative functions of the police, teachers and nurses!

Other trade associations such as the Business Services Association (BSA) and the Independent Healthcare Forum (IHF) carry out similar activities.

New Local Government Network: The Network works with local authorities, government and the private sector to promote elected mayors, localism and modernisation. Its corporate funders include Serco, Jarvis, BT, KPMG, Carillion, Nord Anglia Education PLC, Amey, Sodexho, Capita, Arthur Andersen and a number of other contractors and consultants together with the Confederation of

British Industry. It organises conferences, seminars and issues reports promoting greater private sector involvement in the provision of public services.

The children's services market: The private sector has a vision of children's services providing a stream of lucrative contracts. The DfES commissioned PricewaterhouseCoopers (PwC) to assess the state of the market for children's services and the 'appetite and capacity for expansion' (DfES, 2004). PwC identified 19 services/functions ranging from child care, children's homes, education welfare, school improvement to youth services, Connexions, special schools and special educational needs. The study also identified barriers to entry and suggested ways in which contestability can be extended.

The CBI followed up with a further sector approach to children's services arguing for 'functioning markets' and expressed concern about the sustainability of the market (CBI, 2006). No, not sustainable development but sustainability of profits. They are concerned that 12% and 19% of private providers had very low or low rates of return, although 8% and 40% respectively reported high or reasonable profits from children's services.

British Council for School Environments: To be launched in summer 2006 with 35 founder members including contractors and architects. 'There is a need for the market to respond to the most key moment in school investment in our history' (*Building*, 24 February 2006).

Exporting private finance initiative/public private partnership and growth of the global public private partnership market
● Infrastructure and private finance initiative/public private partnership journals report projects and contracts globally.
● Takeovers and mergers – Spanish takeover of Amey, which has Edinburgh and Glasgow schools private finance initiative contracts. Jarvis sells private finance initiative unit to Hochtieff (Germany).
● Private Prison companies operating internationally
● International bodies promote private finance initiative/public private partnership, and construction companies, banks and other financial institutions, management consultants and other advisers operate internationally.

Examples
Private finance initiative/public private partnership promoted around the world: The Department for International Development and HM

112

Treasury have heavily promoted private finance initiative/public private partnership abroad resulting in a regular flow of public and private sector delegations to Britain to learn the advantages of public/private partnership (and, of course, the experience of Britain's financial institutions, advisers and management consultants).

Network of private finance initiative/public private partnership units: Major contractors, financial institutions, management consultants and legal/technical advisers have established private finance initiative/public private partnership units in key countries to promote projects.

Private finance initiative/public private partnership journals, websites and conferences: The private finance initiative has spawned a number of journals (*PFI Journal, Infrastructure Journal*), web sites and annual conferences which promote the 'success' of the private finance initiative in Britain and overseas, compile league tables, and report on global deals which spur further competition.

World Bank, International Monetary Fund, Development Banks and other agencies promote and fund private finance initiative/public private partnership projects: Studies give favourable slant to private finance initiative/public private partnership infrastructure projects. Global institutions including the United Nations Development Programe, the United Nations Conference on Trade and Development, the United Nations itself, and others make aid packages and projects conditional on the acceptance of public/private partnerships.

World Bank's promotion of private education and outsourcing: Edinvest is an 'education investment facility' for making 'private investment possible on a world scale.' Edinvest promotes the privatisation of education all over the world, and provides technical advice on outsourcing educational services, public private partnerships, and voucher schemes. It is managed by the Centre for British Teachers, a non-profit organisation with OFSTED inspection contracts and school improvement services that owns four day nurseries and uses its annual surplus to promote right-wing education policies overseas.

European Commission Public Private Partnership Green Paper: This paper recognised the wider use of public private partnerships in Europe and focused on how they sit within procurement regulations (EC COM (2004) 327). Although there is no specific Community law governing public private partnerships, they fall within the public contract regulations. The Commission plans an Interpretative Communication in 2006 on 'institutional public private partnerships', ie joint venture companies (EC Press Release IP/05/1440).

Creating consortia and supply chains

● Companies diversify their range of services and enter new markets. Partnerships and consortia will widen and deepen in response to the market, for example Building Schools for the Future consortia will broaden the range of educational services by expanding their supply chain of advisers, consultants and service suppliers through acquisition or organic growth. They will seek to increase their capacity and widen the scope for profit making through stronger control of their supply chain.

● Strategic positioning by forming consortia to bid for contracts, with consolidation in particular sectors such as the supply of agency staff and temporary workers to the public sector, eg teachers and nurses. Rebranding services by setting up new divisions and subsidiaries to demonstrate interest and capacity to undertake public sector work.

● Internal restructuring, for example the redesign of private healthcare services with more flexible packages to insurance companies, selling off smaller units, and ensuring information and communications technology systems are compatible with the public sector, such as the NHS 'choose and book' system.

Examples

Construction companies and financial institutions establish private finance initiative units: All the major construction companies, financial institutions, lawyers and financial advisers have established PFI/PPP units to consolidate activities, submit bids and build capacity.

Diversification into nursery provision: Nord Anglia Education plc originated in language teaching (schools later sold off) and expanded into international schools and private schools in Britain. OFSTED outsourcing of inspection work since 1994 provided a new market and Nord Anglia now inspects 2,718 schools in the north of England and all 387 Further Education and Schools Sixth Forms in England with a £26m four year contract. Nord Anglia diversified into nurseries and now has 102 under the Leapfrog, Jigsaw and Princess Christian brands in addition to local education authority outsourcing, and Department for Education and Skills' and other contracts.

Privatisation of design and technical services through private finance initiative/public private partnerships consortia: The design of public buildings is undertaken almost exclusively by private architects with engineering and technical services also done by private firms. The use of consortia makes private provision the norm – local authorities and public bodies must make a case for public design provision on a case-by-case basis. Building Schools for the Future commenced with 11 exemplar school designs, all by private architects.

Managed services companies establish educational subsidiaries: Many managed services companies – Capita, Serco, HBS, Amey – established educational subsidiaries partly in response to the government's wider use of private companies in 'failing' local education authorities, partly because many contracts included school support services, and companies wanted to demonstrate 'educational' capacity, and partly in response to the continued marketisation and privatisation of state education.

Companies develop diversity of roles: Pace Group – assisting four local authorities on how to respond to Building Schools for the Future, part of the Building Schools for the Future national advisers list, part of a consortia bidding for Building Schools for the Future contracts as educational advisers, part of United Learning Trust – churches group bidding for academies in Manchester and Sheffield. Involved in Building Schools for the Future at every level.

Private sector consortia respond to Building Schools for the Future: Private sector organises consortia including educational and child care consultants, leisure advisers and information and communications technology providers, in addition to traditional private finance initiative consortia members such as construction, finance and facilities management. For example, the Transform Schools consortia includes Balfour Beatty, Haden Building Management (facilities management), Viglen (information and communications technology), Tribal (education services), Innisfree (financial), BDP and Watkins Gray International (architects), Llewelyn Davies Yeang (planning), Avenance (school meals), Strategic Leisure (leisure consultancy) plus other financial and legal advisers.

Privatisation of surgeries: ChilversMcCrea Healthcare was established by a nurse and practising GP in 2001. The firm proposed the concept of corporate General Practice to the Department of Health and now operates General Practices in a number of areas.

Takeovers and mergers
● Takeovers and mergers of other firms and organisations to increase market share and diversify.

Examples
Amey plc (Ferrovial, Spain), Hochtief, (acquired Jarvis private finance initiative unit, Germany), Vinci (France), Skanska (Sweden) are major European and global construction companies, which are bidding for public private partnership infrastructure projects in Britain and elsewhere.

Construction group Carillion plc acquires Mowlem: Carillion's £313m takeover of Mowlem in early 2006 helps to consolidate its position alongside Balfour Beatty as one of Britain's largest construction groups.

Capita Group plc – largest supply teacher agency: Capita systematically built up national presence, mainly through acquisition of smaller companies and agencies.

SERCO acquires ITNET: The IT outsourcing firm ITNET plc was acquired by Serco in February 2005 for £235m. The firm was integrated into Serco and the ITNET name was immediately dropped as it had a chequered history.

Mott MacDonald acquires Cambridge Education Associates (CEA): Mott MacDonald extended its range of consultancy services with the acquisition of Cambridge Education Associates, the major provider of school inspections for OFSTED. Mott MacDonald operates globally in infrastructure, transport, oil and gas, power, water, regeneration, health and other services.

BUPA acquired Associated Nursing Services in August 2005 with 297 residential and nursing homes with 21,000 beds and a £535m annual turnover. US Blackstock buy-in group acquires three UK care firms to topple BUPA as largest operator. Many other chains have been acquired by private equity groups.

Corporate citizen and corporate social responsibility
● Many private firms and markets seek public subsidies through grants, tax concessions on profits, training and labour market concessions, and investment guarantees.

Examples
Reducing red tape and the regulatory burden via Regulatory Impact Assessments: Over 1,000 Regulatory Impact Assessments (RIAs) have been carried out on government policies since 1997. They are designed to assess the implications of public policies on business to try to minimise red tape and market regulations.

Health market turbulence: 'The hip-replacement company Smith & Nephew warned yesterday that the turmoil from Hurricane Katrina would cut sales growth this year. It said that fewer non-essential knee and hip operations in Mississippi and Louisiana would affect profits as a disproportionate amount of sales were there' (*The Guardian*, 14 September 2005). Chief executive Sir Chris O'Donnell said the situation in the southern states was 'very serious' as 'there is a complete dislocation of hospital services, patients and doctors, particularly for elective, non-emergency surgery. We have a relatively strong market share in that part of the southern United States.' (*Telegraph*, 14 September 2005). Smith & Nephew reduced its full year guidance for sales growth for orthopaedics by 1% to 17%. Its shares fell 6% or 34.5 pence to 509 pence on the sales warning.

European Union Internal Market for Services: Draft Services Directive for liberalisation of services – see Chapter 2.

World Trade Organisation, General Agreement on Trade in Services: Proposals for liberalisation of services – see Chapter 2.

The continuation of the marketisation strategy, has profound implications and lasting for the role of the state and urban governance. It has little to do with modernisation in the traditional sense and everything to do with implementing and embedding neo-liberalism.

If local authorities and public bodies, in future, commission all services but provide few, this will have a significant knock-on effect on the organisation and purpose of local government and other public bodies. The possible fragmentation of local government into separate Children's Services, Adult Services, Community/environmental services trusts or arms length organisations, each with 'local elections' and partnerships, will be countered by the case for the creation of new City Regions (Office of the Deputy Prime Minister, 2006). If transnational companies are now members of the 'NHS family' (Blair, February 2006), then they will no doubt become members of the local government 'family'. Partnership is apparently to be superseded by a more 'familiar' relationship.

Local authorities should, in theory, become strategic regulators ensuring that '... the market works to the benefit of all local residents; value for money is obtained through procurement and commissioning; choice is informed and is exercised; there is sufficient capacity to make choice real; there is fair access to the market and no discrimination; and outcomes are at least as equitable as under monopoly provision' (IPPR, 2005). There will also be '... moves toward market-making, assurance and modernised audit, and away from detailed inspection' (ibid). It will be alleged, of course, to be mere coincidence that, just when the private sector takes over responsibility for service provision, the case for detailed inspection vanishes!

The reality of this fantasy world will be quite different. Local and central government will cease to be major employers. The market will determine staffing levels, terms and conditions. Public sector trade unionism will be a thing of the past. Commissioning will be exposed for what it is – contract management. Planning and needs assessment functions will be marginalised as the contract culture becomes pervasive and resources are sucked into managing contracts, coordinating contractors and arbitrating disputes. But 'market-making' will provide academics and consultants with lots of 'research' money to ponder why equity, fair access and non-discrimination have been 'neglected'.

There will be a substantial shift in power from the public to the private sector. Corporate welfare will be embedded in public services and the welfare state. Marketisation is not intended to create patient-led hospitals and health centres nor pupil/parent-led schools any more than 'participation' is intended to empower community organisations. The reality is that depoliticisation and disillusionment with political institutions could be even more extensive creating the conditions for instability and community conflict.

The public sector faces further years of crisis and conflict as a result of New Labour's modernisation by marketisation strategy. There is no certainty that any of their marketisation plans will 'work' because they are not based on evidence but ideology.

The limitations of a service-by-service opposition, be it health, education, social care, housing or regeneration, should be evident. Campaigns will inevitably be rooted in particular services, but they must be broadened to address neo-liberal ideology, develop alternative strategies and avoid getting sidetracked into Parliamentary clauses or the meaning of phrases in letters between Secretaries of State and MPs.

CHAPTER 7

The public cost of marketisation

Winners and losers

Despite the spin, there is no such thing as a win-win scenario. Economic law and political science theory constantly show that there are both winners and losers. With regard to marketisation, the key questions are, who gets paid for work carried out in the marketisation process? What are the costs, and who bears the cost of these payments? It is equally important to ask who benefits and who loses? What could have been provided instead?

The winners and losers in the marketisation process are summarised in Table 9.

Public sector costs

Marketisation incurs substantial costs in setting-up new organisations, transferring assets and services to arms length organisations and private and voluntary organisations, and in managing the procurement process. The public sector incurs a wide range of costs ranging from the appraisal of options and market sounding, preparation of specifications and contract documents, the cost of the procurement process including advertising and legal and financial advisers fees, contract negotiation costs, and client and contract management costs. In some circumstances the costs are claimed to be nil, because they are deferred or shunted to another budget heading, but are still borne by the public sector. The full costs are rarely quantified.

The costs identified in Table 10 are only the public sector costs. Private and voluntary organisations incur substantial transaction costs in bidding for contracts. These become the 'cost of doing business' and are in effect reflected in their overall costs, which are borne by all the organisations to whom they supply services. There are also significant social, economic, health, environmental and sustainable development impacts.

Marketisation is a massive drain on the public sector. All the costs identified below are a diversion of resources from frontline provision.

Table 9: *Winners and losers in marketisation*

Who was paid for what	What are the costs	Who bears the costs
Construction companies Facilities management contractors Managed services and other private contractors Consultants & financial, legal and technical advisers Banks and financial institutions for funding privately financed projects.	Transfer of organisations and assets Cost of competition and contestability Cost of management consultants Cost of Regulation **Total: £8,355m one-off costs to date plus £3,097m annual costs**	Service users Council tenants Council taxpayers Taxpayers in general for marketisation of NHS, civil services, agencies, public bodies and partly for local authorities.

Who loses	*Who benefits*	*What could have been provided (the opportunity costs)*
Service users and potential users. Council tenants Public sector employees (a few gain, but most do not) Equalities groups.	Private companies and construction/Facilities management firms. Management consultants, financial and legal advisers Public sector chief executives and senior managers get higher wages. Shareholders and investment companies Banks and financial institutions Some service users benefit who have the skills and experience to take advantage of market system. Government/Treasury – taxes paid by companies, contractors and taxes on profits and dividends.	The public money spent on marketisation could have: * Built 200 Children's Centres with running costs for 10 years. * £5bn could have financed the 4th option for council housing and improved 835,000 homes to Decent Homes Standard. * Increased expenditure by £50m in the 20 most deprived neighbourhoods. * Provided annual health screening for 5m people for 10 years. * Built 100 multi-purpose sports centres with running costs for 5 years.

Table 10: *The Public Cost of Marketisation*

Type of costs incurred	On-off costs (£m)	Annual cost (£m)
Transfer of organisations and assets Large Scale Voluntary Transfer (LSVT) programme transferred 943,485 council homes in England up to November 2005 (ODPM, 2005). National Audit Office calculated cost of hypothetical 1m home 5-year transfer programme to be £4.2 billion over 30 years (£4,200 per home). (Costs to date include £389m set-up costs, Gap funding of £75.6m and overhanging debt of £1,720m) 943,485 x £3,200 to take account of phasing of transfer programme over longer period.	3,019	
Planned stock transfers of 50,000 per annum @ £4,200		**210**
Arms Length Management Organisations (ALMOs) for council housing – set up, office and transfer costs: 30 x £0.5m	**15**	
Set up costs for 50 Leisure Trusts x £400,000 (evidence from Trust projects)	**20**	
Set up costs for 22 Urban Regeneration Companies and 5 Urban Development Corporations @ £0.5m	**13.5**	
Set up costs for x Foundation Hospitals – £300,000 (est)	**9.6**	
x 32 (Department of Health nor the independent regulator, Monitor, hold information on the administrative costs of foundation trust status, Hansard Written Answer, 3 November 2005, col 1337W). Cost of further 50 Foundation Trusts.	**15**	
Establishing Trust schools (to own assets, employ staff, procure services and operate admissions) 1,500 x £100,000 legal, financial and other costs.	**150**	
Cost of choice, competition and contestability Bonus incentives for Patient Choice	**95**	
Cost of patient choice at referral – annual infrastructure costs of choose and book plus annual cost for PCTs (NAO, 2005). Efficiencies are claimed to offset these costs but 'none of these benefits will necessarily enable cash to be released' (ibid)		**122**
Payment by Results in NHS additional costs (Audit Commission, 2005).	**50**	
NHS outsourcing of £3bn elective surgery included 15% premium for private sector set-up and investment costs.	**450**	

Type of costs incurred	On-off costs (£m)	Annual cost (£m)
Virtual money box pilot scheme for individual budgets for older and disabled people (DH press release 21 November 2005)	2.6	
Additional building cost of Academies – average DfES contribution to building cost £22,070 based on 27 projects and £596m cost (Hansard 13 December 2005 col 1891W) less average cost of secondary school of £12.5m = £10m x 200 planned academies.	2,000	
Competitions for establishment of new schools – £50,000 (est) x 50 annually		2.5
Choice advisors for schools – £6m per annum (Education and Skills Committee Report, 2006) plus cost of care brokers, job brokers, zone agents and other market intermediaries.		15
Social HomeBuy – local authority and council tenants can purchase a minimum equity share in home, based on 5,000 sales per annum and cost of reimbursing housing associations for discounts (Final RIA, Home Buy, ODPM, 2005)		30
Right to Buy – replacing a dwelling sold through this programme produces a net financial cost to government of £15,000 per dwelling (Final RIA, HomeBuy, ODPM, 2005). UK local authority housebuilding completions have been 301, 207 and 131 between 2002/3 and 2004/5. Government policy now to encourage local authority/ALMO housebuilding so assume 500 new homes per annum (£15,000 x 500)		7.5
Additional cost of PFI/PPP projects: 740 signed projects with capital costs of £47bn – 'private sector's weighted cost of finance, both debt and equity together, is typically between 1% and 3% higher than public sector's cost of debt on a non-risk adjusted basis' (PwC, 2005). Assume average 2% plus 2% higher transaction costs (Accounts Commission Scotland (careful re capital and total costs)	1,880	
Additional costs of PFI/PPP projects currently at planning and procurement stages – £11,583m capital value of projects at preferred bidder stage with expected financial close by 2006/07 (HM Treasury, 2005). Plus projects at earlier stages of procurement = total of £6bn per annum x 4% higher cost. (Dept of Health revenue support for PFI scheme, all projects above £25m will receive 7.5% of capital value over 5 years and NHS		240

Type of costs incurred	On-off costs (£m)	Annual cost (£m)
Bank will contribute 2% of total scheme cost – Reform, 2005)		
PFI/PPP units established in government departments (estimate based on departmental web sites)		5
PFI supplement paid to some NHS Trusts because of affordability problems (£45m to UCL)		45
Building Schools for the Future (LEP set-up costs £0.5m x 160 education authorities in England (additional PFI costs included in PFI section above).	80	
Partnerships for Schools (DfES quango) 45 staff and still recruiting		3.5
Centre for Procurement Performance in DfES (est)		0.5
Partnerships for Health (DH quango) responsible for NHS LIFT		3.5
Office for Government Commerce, part of operating costs devoted to promoting outsourcing, PPP and strategic partnerships.		5
Decent Homes options appraisal, consultants, consultation in 280 local authorities, excluding those who transferred prior to end 2002 (England) x £0.5m est. average cost	140	
Commissioning and procurement of services in local government. Additional client/commissioning and contract management costs related to procurement and competition estimated to be 5% of contract value (11% procurement and contract management costs in civil service (Cabinet Office, 1996) and 6.2% contract management costs (DoE, 1993). UK local government expenditure of £89.8bn in 2004/5 on pay, goods and services (PESA Table 6.10, 2005). Assume £10bn outsourcing services.		500
Commissioning and procurement of services in NHS – £2.3bn competitive tendering in 185 organisations with £795m outsourced (NHS PASA, 2003). Assume increase to £6bn based on 5% costs – see above.		300
Commissioning and procurement of services in government departments and agencies: Administration costs £20bn (PESA Table 5.1, 2005). Assume £4bn based on 5% costs – see above.		200

Type of costs incurred	On-off costs (£m)	Annual cost (£m)
Commissioning and procurement of services in 211 Non-Departmental Public Bodies with £32.9bn gross expenditure 2003/4. Assume £5bn based on 5% costs – see above.		250
Prison and Probation contestability programme for National Offender Management System – based on competition costs for new prisons £1.1m per prison, market testing prisons £0.7m, performance testing prisons £0.35m, market testing 42 probation areas £12.5m, contract compliance £2.1m and contract management costs of 1.2% = total cost £17m per minimum for 25 years = £425m (NOMS Partial RIA, November 2005). NOMS set up costs estimated to be £5m of £289m NOMS headquarters costs in 2005/6 (includes contracted prisons).	5	17
Capacity building in voluntary sector to bid for contracts – £150m capacity builders programme and £215m Futurebuilders fund to encourage third sector bidding for public service contracts (HM Treasury, 2005).	365	
Increased capacity costs in edcation, health and other services. This will include the cost of extra infrastructure costs of schools and health facilities plus the cost of spare capacity in some existing facilities. Increased capacity in education – 2% of secondary school expenditure £12.6bn in 2003/04 (DfES Annual Report 2004) and 2% of NHS elective care expenditure £8.7bn in 2003/04 (NAO, 2005) adjusted for inflation to 2005/06.		470
Housing Market Renewal Pathfinders – cost of 9 projects and public capital investment, £20m and £170m in 2004/05 with total investment of £1bn between 2005/06 and 2007/08. Does not include private sector investment.		120
Cost of management consultants Public sector spent £1.9bn on management consultancy in 2004 withoutsourcing accounting for 39% of fee income – all sectors (MCA, 2005). Assume 20% expenditure on reviews, procurement, commissioning and outsourcing to avoid double counting of PFI/PPP consultancy.		380

Type of costs incurred	On-off costs (£m)	Annual cost (£m)
Cost of Regulation		
Cost of Regulation offices – postal services, rail, gas and electricity, water and communications (Postcomm, ORR, OFGEM, OFWAT and OFCOM annual reports)		210
Cost of 9 Regional Centres of Excellence @ £400,000 pa (ODPM, 2005).		3.6
Miscellaneous costs		2
Additional research into market mechanisms and impacts		112
Total cost	**8,355.7**	**3,097**

Note: Efficiency savings claims are usually exaggerated, government research in 1990s found between 6.5% – 8.0% savings (DoE 1993 and 1997) but when all public sector costs are taken into account the savings disappear with a negative –16.0% cost to government (Equal Opportunities Commission, 1995 and Centre for Public Services 1995). Claims of savings and value for money from PPP and outsourcing but no evidence to substantiate claims based on comparable projects, contexts and comprehensive impact assessments.

CHAPTER 8

The impact of marketisation and market failure

This chapter briefly examines the potential implications of marketisation on public services, employment, social justice, democratic accountability and civil society. The expansion of markets and competition in public services is usually justified on the basis that this will improve the quality of services – that the rigours of competition will ultimately produce more effective and efficient services. In practice, some users benefit, but this is usually at the expense of others. More importantly, the imposition of markets and competition leads to structural changes, which have a fundamental impact on social justice, democratic governance, employment and the welfare state.

The impact of marketisation is assessed on:
● Crises, closures, fragmentation, and diversion of public resources
● Loss of democratic accountability and transparency
● Less sustainable development
● Eroding social justice and equalities
● Public domain
● Outsourcing, offshoring and weaker trade unions
● The impact on cities and regions
● Increasing corporate power
● Market failure

Crises, closures, fragmentation, and diversion of public resources

Erosion of public service principles and values: Core public service principles and values such as objectivity, accountability, selflessness, leadership and safeguarding the public interest are eroded and replaced by narrow operational business and commercial values.

Failure to plan for social needs: Markets do not plan for social needs – they do so only to the extent that it is in the market's self interest to 'plan' and address social needs. Research and planning for public services rests with the state (much of the research is increasingly outsourced) but since public bodies have less and less technical know-how, skills, and experience of service delivery, they have reduced capacity to undertake the work to the scope and quality required. The failed £1.1bn private finance initiative Paddington Health Campus in

126

London is a classic example of the consequences of market megalomania overriding social need and rational planning. The North West London Strategic Health Authority wasted £14m on the project, forcing it to undertake a major rationalisation of services.

Capacity of the state and intellectual capital: Marketisation and privatisation are systematically reducing the ability of the state to carry out the core functions of the nation state, to intervene in markets and to plan social and economic progress.

Public resources diverted for private gain: Public resources and skills are used to promote private interests and profits rather than help to meet social needs. For example, civil servants and public officials spend an increasing part of their time creating and sustaining markets.

Loss of economies of scale: Public sector economies of scale are eroded by the transfer, fragmentation and outsourcing of services, resulting in fewer frontline services using central support services. Value for money achieved by providing central services (such as human resources, payroll, financial and legal services) switches from the public to the private sector as contractors win more contracts and are able to spread their costs to achieve economies of scale.

Hospitals and schools face financial crisis: Hospitals and schools will be confronted with financial deficits as a result of competition and markets – hospitals will face having to repay existing deficits, achieve efficiency savings, adjust to the loss of income as elective surgery is transferred to private sector treatment centres, and primary care trusts press for more community care. The private sector will cherry-pick or cream-skim the easiest and cheapest cases, park the complex patients and pupils with the NHS and the local education authority, and avoid responsibility for training, research and addressing the public sector's corporate policies and priorities. Although the NHS as a whole broke even in 2003/04, the number of organisations in deficit rose 6% to 18% (National Audit Office and Audit Commission, 2005).

Public resources are diverted to funding consultants and advertising agencies: A larger slice of public resources is consumed by middle agents such as consultants, recruitment firms and advertising agencies because hospitals and schools are no longer part of large public sector organisations from which they can draw advice and experience. They also want to chart their own way forward and will increasingly have to advertise to attract patients and parents – so will hire their own management consultants, agencies and advisers.

Closure of schools and hospitals: Marketisation means that poor performing or 'failing' NHS hospitals and local education authority schools could eventually close, as patients and pupils choose to attend other hospitals and schools and funding follows to the new school or hospital. Closures are likely to be preceded by a period of private sector management attempting to improve performance and impose more commercial management, thus limiting those personal 'choices' promised.

Contract failures and terminations: There have been systemic failures such as Railtrack and British Energy and a series of partnership and contract failures as well as company failures. For example, the Bedfordshire County Council and West Berkshire Council Strategic Service-Delivery Partnerships were terminated in 2005, twenty area rail maintenance contracts were terminated in 2004, the London Borough of Southwark terminated its education contract with WS Atkins, and Capita's Individual Learning Accounts project failed in 2002 because of the high level of abuse. There have been many contract terminations for individual services such as hospital cleaning. Three private finance initiative contractors have had financial crises – Ballast, Jarvis and Amey. The latter survived through a takeover by a Spanish construction company. Following the failings of a series of multi-million pound private finance initiative information technology contracts, the government announced that PFI would no longer be used for such projects.

Despite evidence of crises and failures by the private sector, such as the London Underground public private partnership project, this is sometimes turned around and the public sector blamed. 'The Northern line problem is not necessarily a failure of the private sector, but of the public sector's ability to understand how to manage its relationships with the private sector' (letter to *The Guardian*, 20 October 2005, from the Director, Institute of Local Government Studies, University of Birmingham).

Public sector forced to repair private failure: Patients requiring emergency/intensive care in private hospitals are frequently transferred for treatment in NHS hospitals. The NHS also has to deal with the mistakes made by cowboy cosmetic surgeons – a study by the Royal Free and Chelsea and Westminster hospitals in London reported that in one year 50 private cosmetic patients required NHS treatment (*Financial Times*, 19 October 2005).

Poor design: A design review of 13 of the 17 private finance initiative schools for South Lanarkshire Council by Architecture and Design Scotland cited cramped layouts, the organisation of accommodation around central 'streets' as little more than glorified corridors, and 'scant evidence of any kind of architectural vision' (minutes of design review meeting, 10 May 2005). The findings echoed earlier reports from the Educational Institute of Scotland, Audit Scotland and the Audit Commission on private finance initiative schools.

Fragmentation and division: The complexity of planning and operating across geographic and organisational boundaries, with public sector organisations having different levels and systems of accountability, different funding regimes, different corporate objectives and priorities, and different targets and performance management frameworks, makes joint working difficult. Marketisation will make this more difficult by imposing a network of contracts, and the separation of strategic policymaking and service delivery, with more organisations operating at arms length.

Loss of flexibility: Contracts are inflexible and it is usually very costly to negotiate major amendments to contracts and/or to issue more than a minimal number of variation orders. Public bodies lose a degree of flexibility in responding to changing needs, circumstances and/or emergencies.

Growth of private markets have costs and consequences for public services: Private health screening is a fast growing market, but a recent British Medical Association study highlighted the limitations of many tests. 'Whole body scanning' which can result in false alarms, leading to unnecessary, invasive tests, and false negatives where disease is not detected (BMA, 2005). Doctors are concerned that NHS resources are diverted to providing further tests and counselling for the 'worried well' (*Financial Times*, 24 August 2005).

The threat to core services: how teachers were corralled
Education demonstrates very clearly how a core service can become highly vulnerable to outsourcing and privatisation (see Figure 3). The teaching profession has been encircled by different forms of marketisation and privatisation to such an extent that it now makes the position of teachers highly vulnerable. The private provision of supply teachers, academies, the increasing outsourcing of educational support services, privately financed school buildings, and privately controlled Local Education Parnerships in the Building Schools for the Future programme preceded government plans for schools to

become trusts employing their own staff, owning schools and playing fields and managing admissions.

The ramifications of these policies have yet to be fully understood. Local bargaining could have a major impact on teachers' pay and conditions. But more is at stake – the privatisation of a public good. Secondary and primary education may remain largely state funded for the foreseeable future, but they will be delivered mainly by private contractors. The futility of relying on vested interest 'professionalism', and the failure to take appropriate action when related services and functions were being marketised and privatised, should be starkly apparent.

Figure 3:
The marketisation of education: How teachers were corralled

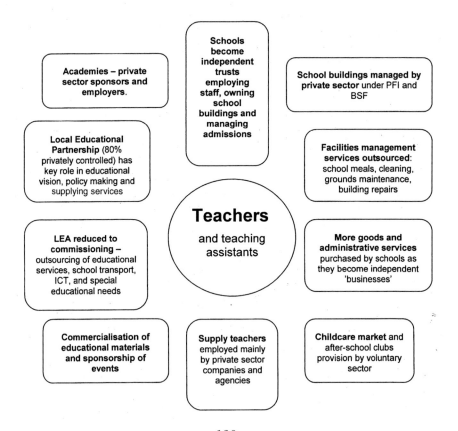

Loss of democratic accountability and transparency

Democratic accountability and public governance marginalised:
Marketisation results in more services being delivered by the private
sector, arms length companies and trusts, which erodes democratic
accountability. Private companies are responsible for the performance
of contracts according to the terms of their contract with public
bodies, but this is only one element of accountability. Private firms are
accountable to shareholders and, in some cases, to regulatory bodies
for market activities and prices. Elected members on the boards of
arms length companies and trusts have a legal responsibility to the
company, which takes precedence over their public responsibilities.

Participatory democracy: Marketisation imposes a particular form of
participation on community and civil society organisations which is
essentially focused on representation on arms length boards and
trusts. It rarely addresses the demands for greater involvement in the
planning, design and implementation of public policy.

Simplistic analysis, rhetoric and damned lies: 'For over 60 years the
power in health in this country has lain with the providers. I am going
to transfer power to the patients', stated John Reid, then Secretary of
State for Health (*Financial Times*, 3 February 2005). Power is in fact
being transferred to another set of providers – private health care
firms.

Transparency reduced: 'Commercial confidentiality' is the norm as
public bodies strictly apply procurement regulations and the private
sector becomes even more secretive to retain its commercial
advantage. The exemptions under the Freedom of Information Act
2000 are likely to maintain high levels of secrecy. Corporate financial
reporting requirements are virtually irrelevant to gaining information
concerning investment strategies, supply chains, subcontractor
relationships, employment practices and contract performance.

Competition or single bidders when it suits: Private finance initiative
competition is reducing. Previously, there had to be a minimum of
three bidders. Then the £750m St Bartholomew's and Royal London
Hospitals scheme had only two bidders. Recently, the Balfour Beatty-
Canmore Properties consortium was appointed preferred bidder for
the £190m Stobhill and Victoria Hospital in Glasgow, despite no other
rival bids. There are two other major hospital schemes in Plymouth
(£340m Derriford project) and East London (£350m Whipps Cross)
with only one bidder awaiting a government response to proceed or
re-tender. Single-bid contracts contravene the public sector

131

procurement regulations and make the demonstration of value for money extremely difficult.

Less sustainable development

Limiting sustainable production and supply chains: Marketisation imposes financial cost pressures leading to national and international sourcing of goods and services by multinational companies to maximise cost advantages and profits. This fractures local and regional production and supply chains as 'financial savings' override sustainable development, local employment and regional economy priorities.

Reducing sustainable development standards: Public sector standards will be eroded and replaced by private sector corporate social responsibility standards. Local authorities have encountered difficulties ensuring private contractors implement council corporate policies and priorities. Implementation of sustainable development policies will be even more difficult. Contractors are likely to introduce more market-based trade-offs, such as compensating activities and negative impacts in Britain by planting of forests in other parts of Europe, which can only be inspected and verified at high cost.

Less sustainable economy: Building a strong, stable and sustainable economy which provides prosperity and opportunities for all is at odds with increased reliance on market forces for basic human needs such as health and education. Markets have not got a strong track record in meeting the diverse needs of all people in existing communities, promoting personal wellbeing, social cohesion and inclusion, and creating equal opportunity for all.

More limited impact assessment: The private sector has a long track record of avoiding taking responsibility for social and environmental costs. Impact assessments are rarely comprehensive and often put shareholder interests before respect for the limits of the planet's environment, resources and biodiversity.

Erosion of social justice and equalities

Transferring the risk to staff: Outsourcing effectively means that public sector workers, not the client, are being forced to bare the risk of changes to terms and conditions of service, changes to workplace conditions, and changes to staff consultation and representation. The level of risk identified with a set of criteria in an Employment Risk Matrix range from none, low, medium to high. Secondment of staff has 19% in the no-risk and 81% in the low risk category compared to

48% and 33% respectively in the high and medium risk category in a TUPE staff transfer (Centre for Public Services, 2005).

Increasing inequalities: Marketisation will create new inequalities in service delivery and workplaces, particularly with respect to access, affordability, employment (widening wage differentials), and quality of service. Tackling existing inequalities will be more difficult.

Whilst core public services may remain free at the point of use, commercialisation will require users to pay for 'optional extras' such as information and communication technology facilities and better quality food, thus creating issues of affordability. There will also be differences in access to information because information about choices and providers depends on access to information and communication technology. Levels of education and language also determine ability to understand the implications of the information accessed.

In addition, equality groups are also likely to experience the consequences of the gaming techniques practised by private sector service providers such as 'parking'.

Equity markets: Exploitation of public resources by creating a secondary market in private finance initiative project equity means that gains in the value of what should be public assets, since they are paid for entirely by taxpayers, are instead expropriated by the private sector.

New avenues of exploitation are created: Moves towards creating an asset-based welfare system will open up new avenues of exploitation. For example, in the United States patients with health care debts have had to sell their homes or have them repossessed – Yale hospital owned 2,000 houses in 2004 as a result of health debt. A new 'business service' is created to deal with patient debt. The longer term consequences of asset-based welfare are deliberately ignored by the advocates of such policies. The sale of council housing in Britain led to property companies and loan sharks, culminating in regulations to try to limit their activities.

Commercialising the community and voluntary sector: Marketisation encourages the voluntary sector to bid for public service contracts and, in some cases, to adopt empire-building strategies. The government is so keen to have a competitive voluntary sector that it has funded a capacity building programme and is heavily promoting the sector's potential role in the delivery of public services. Voluntary organisations inevitably have to adopt more commercial practices in order to compete alongside the private sector in the procurement process.

Community benefits: Particular phrases become associated with specific marketisation and privatisation policies. 'Community benefit' has common currency because of the mainstreaming of procurement. It is now expected that procurement should produce community benefits such as local training and employment in addition to the services or works being tendered for. So 'community benefit' becomes synonymous with procurement, and officers debate how well they have done relative to others, and how 'innovative' they have been in operating within the European procurement regulations. Research is commissioned to identify 'best practice', and the extension of community benefits to service delivery is promoted, instead of being limited to works contracts! Yet in-house services have been producing community benefits for years, without being branded as such. Direct service organisations have apprentice training schemes, and other local authority services have had employment schemes for many years.

The European procurement regulations, based on the concept of a single competitive market, mean that evasive language must be used to identify at whom the 'community benefits' are targeted. To state this openly would conflict with the regulations! Markets clearly create absurdity.

Public domain

More privatisation: Further privatisation of public assets is almost certain to follow the marketisation of services. As the private sector gains an increasing share of the delivery of a service, it will also have a greater role in public policy making and the use of assets. Markets will inevitably grow so that a larger part, if not all, of the service is marketised. This will be 'justified' in the name of economies of scale and value for money. The process usually involves the privatisation of assets, leaving any unprofitable or complex functions for the state.

Outsourcing, offshoring and weaker trade unions

Job losses: Although the Transfer of Undertakings (Protection of Employment) Regulations 1981 (TUPE) and the Code of Practice on Workforce Matters provide a degree of security for transferred employees, job losses usually occur in the rationalisation process running parallel to the procurement process. Leaving or retiring staff are replaced by temporary staff. Offshoring results in a direct loss of jobs in the local and regional economy (see www.centre.public.org.uk/outsourcing-library).

Pensions: There are significant differences in the quality of public and private sector pensions with the private sector rapidly replacing final salary schemes with money purchase schemes. This represents a significant loss of income for both the individuals and the local economy.

Terms and conditions: Markets and the procurement process leads to increased competition between employers on staffing levels, working practices and terms and conditions, and in a globalising economy, where different parts of the service will be produced. The Best Value Code of Practice on Workforce Matters requires only that terms and conditions are 'broadly comparable' which leaves scope for differences between pay rates, pensions, sick pay and holidays between new and transferred staff to emerge over time.

Trade union organisation and representation: Workplace organisation and representation is becoming more fragmented both nationally and locally. The proportion of employees in trade unions in the public sector is nearly three times higher than in the private sector (64% compared to 22% according to the 2004 Workplace Employment Relations Survey). Locally, many public sector trade union branches organise, represent and negotiate with an increasing variety of employers in the public, private and voluntary sectors. This can fragment resources, dilute responses and widen agendas thus forcing more selective action.

The impact on cities and regions

Potential impact on regional economy: Most Regional Economic Strategies belatedly recognise the economic importance of the public sector. However, marketisation reduces the potential for regionally based innovation, service development, and business formation, and weakens the city region concept. The private sector will focus on national and international markets with contracts being operated on similar lines to a branch plant economy with few new jobs, imported contract management, wider use of labour from Eastern Europe, centralised support services, national and international sourcing of goods and services, and the export of profits out of the regional economy.

City regions: The idea behind city regions is to increase economic and political power to create more competitive and sustainable cities. However, continued marketisation of public services (the public sector accounts for up to 30% of employment in many cities) will undermine this concept as ownership of assets and supply chains will increasingly be controlled by transnational companies.

Increasing corporate power

Business involvement in public policy making: Most contractors are members of business organisations and trade associations which are part of national and global networks that campaign to minimise regulation and create the best possible climate and conditions to 'do business'. This includes intensive lobbying of the European Union and World Trade Organisation promoting liberalisation of public services. They also help to fund right-wing think tanks, political parties and candidates.

Public provision replaced by private monopoly: Outsourcing frequently leads to less competition as a handful of firms eventually dominate each sector through takeovers and mergers and the use of market power. Some private finance initiative projects do not obtain even the minimum number of bidders.

Risk of collusion: Collusion is most likely to occur when there 'are a small number of bidders, so that it is easy to organise a cartel, and there are barriers to entry that prevent new supplies, outside of the cartel, from bidding' (Department of Trade and Industry, 2005). It can also occur when 'there are a number of very similar contracts so that potential suppliers can share the contracts between each other in the expectation that each will generate similar profits' (ibid).

Corporate social responsibility and corporate citizen roles: Whilst some companies, agencies and academics claim that corporate social responsibility is a very effective way of persuading business to take responsibility for the economic, social and environmental impacts of their activities, there is also another school of thought which believes that business must fully respect all human rights, labour, environmental mandates and regulations, and not get 'rewarded' for doing so. Regulatory regimes should be much more comprehensive, with action taken against non-compliance.

Corporate welfare complex: Marketisation reinforces the four pillars of a corporate welfare complex, in particular the contract services system, the owner-operator infrastructure industry, and the corporatisation of public bodies. The separation of strategic policy and service delivery, together with continued state withdrawal from service delivery, will provide new opportunities for the private sector to build more powerful business associations and lobby groups to represent their interests. They will use their muscle to influence the policy-making, financing and regulation of service provision. The contract services system and owner-operator infrastructure industry constitute a powerful lobby which will almost certainly influence regulatory regimes and set the parameters of debate and public policy. Consortia are likely to expand into services and activities outside the scope of the Regulator whilst also making demands on the state for subsidies, grants and favourable payment systems.

More corruption: A contract culture with ever larger sums of money at stake inevitably creates pressures and opportunities for different forms of corruption, ranging from payments to gifts and services- in-kind.

Market failure

There have been many examples of contract failures and more systemic market failures (see page 128).

CHAPTER 9

An alternative modernisation strategy

There is an alternative to modernisation by marketisation and to the negative impacts and drastic consequences summarised in the previous chapter. This chapter sets out the central themes and core policies of an Alternative Modernisation Strategy. It should be part of a wider economic and social strategy for Britain. The next chapter makes the case for public provision and delivery.

Central themes
● Restatement of public service principles and values which are embedded in all policies, programmes and projects.
● Democratic accountability and transparency including a revitalisation and empowerment of local government.
● Integration of strategic policy making and service provision with the abolition of the commissioning/outsourcing agenda.
● Long term planning for social needs.
● Better horizontal and vertical integration of local, regional and national public bodies.
● Equalities, social justice and sustainable development mainstreamed.
● Integrated impact assessment of policies, programmes and projects required at planning and implementation stages.
● Increased capacity of local and central government and public bodies, drastically reducing the use of management consultants.
● Quality employment and a better skilled workforce, with education, training and learning, workforce development, and good quality pensions.

Core policies
An alternative modernisation agenda would include:
   National and regional planning – New national economic and spatial strategy with designated growth strategies developed for each region. Integration of investment strategies, innovation, research, knowledge transfer, cluster development, and local/regional production and supply chains to maximise local employment and more sustainable economies.
   Increased public investment in the infrastructure and termination of the Private Finance Initiative (including NHS Local Improvement

Finance Trust and Building Schools for the Future) and Strategic Service-delivery Partnerships.

Refocus on social justice and reducing inequalities through redistribution and targeting together with equality impact assessment of all policies and projects. Comprehensive equality legislation covering all equality strands.

Democratic accountability, participation and transparency to include:
● Local government to takeover responsibility for primary care and public health.
● Democratisation of the NHS and regional bodies and abolition of Foundation status for hospitals.
● Return all quangos, arms length companies and trusts within the framework of local government.
● Genuine user/employee and community organisation/trade union participation in the policy making process, together with additional resources for community organising and fuller disclosure of information. Community and voluntary organisations to be involved in the design, planning and evaluation of public policy instead of being coerced into service provision.
● Harness potential of information and communications technology to widen community access, e-citizenship and e-democracy.
● Replace business domination of task forces, arms length companies and other organisations with elected members and wide community representation.

Public sector consortia or lead-authority concept to develop joint approach to information and communications technology and corporate service provision for local authorities, health and other public bodies where desirable, using secondment employment model and democratic, accountable organisational structures.

Abolition of market based mechanisms in education, health, social care and other services including the removal of competition and procurement requirements. Service Improvement Plans, agreed and monitored by Elected Members, users and trade unions, to serve as basis for in-house service provision.

More radical approach to sustainable development: A new sustainable development framework for national and international action devoid of the liberalisation agenda, new standards for sustainability, emphasis on local and regional production and supply chains.

Extensive training programme in public service principles and values to reinvigorate public service management and the implementation of an alternative modernisation strategy,

Choice and flexibility in the public sector: Increased choice is possible within public services by extending and expanding in-house services, and using spare capacity and peaks and troughs to widen choice without establishing markets. Choice with collective empowerment exercised with other users is more powerful and meaningful than individual market-based choice. Abolition of market based mechanisms.

New public service management: Replace competitions for pilots and pathfinders by planned and negotiated projects which are fully evaluated before they are mainstreamed.

Re-regulation of markets to address social needs, increase public control, and improve environmental, health and safety, economic, and sustainable development benefits.

Genuine community schools with child care, health, adult learning, leisure and other local services operating extended hours.

Implementation of the 4ᵗʰ option for Council Housing with immediate additional public investment and the transfer of arms length management organisations back to local authorities.

National Public Transport Plan rebalancing rail/bus transport and road building with new investment in inter-city and local public transport.

Opposition to the World Trade Organisation General Agreement on Trade in Services liberalisation proposals: Demand exclusion of public services and welfare state functions together with strengthening of adherence to human rights and labour regulations.

Remain vigilant on how the modified European Union Services Directive is drawn up and reflects the agreed compromises.

CHAPTER 10

Why public provision is essential

In-house provision of public services is both advantageous and essential and makes a substantial contribution to community well-being, liveability, sustainable development and social justice. The case is made under the following headings:
- Improving community well-being
- Democratic accountability
- Equalities and social justice
- Sustainable development
- Protecting the public interest
- Financial advantages
- Corporate policies
- Better quality employment
- Capacity

Improving community well-being

Coordination and integration of services and functions: Service delivery, social inclusion, community well-being strategies, regeneration, and economic development increasingly require a multidisciplinary, coordinated approach. This requires integrated teams, the pooling of skills, experience and resources between directorates and organisations in networks, partnerships, alliances and coalitions with the public sector playing a central role. It requires joined-up government, not quasi joined-up contracts. The objective is to achieve the vertical and horizontal integration of a democratically accountable and complex range of services.

Improving community well-being: Recent research has demonstrated that improved performance and productivity requires five key elements – engaging and motivating staff, meeting service users needs, promoting creativity and innovation, keeping stakeholders involved and informed, and increasing shareholder value (improving community well being in public services) – being managed and coordinated. 'Managing them in isolation impairs performance' (Will Hutton, *Financial Times*, 17 November 2003). Contracts fragment service delivery, replicating the very 'silos' which modernisation is supposed to be eliminating.

Integration of strategic policy and service delivery: Identifying, assessing and prioritising social needs, as well as planning and allocating resources and operational management, are integral to the quality of

141

service. Close working between client and contractor is essential to improve services and ensure that they address social needs.

Continuity and security: Continuity of service and knowledge of local requirements and conditions are important parts of service delivery. For many service users, particularly the elderly, security and continuity of service delivery are an important part of the quality of service. In-house provision provides longer-term security of provision.

Maximising scope for improvement: Integration and coordination with other services achieves economies of scale, cost sharing and improved service quality.

Better quality of service: Properly resourced in-house services can provide a higher standard of service, and are more responsive and flexible to changing needs and circumstances.

Working to needs, not to contracts and profits: The prime purpose of in-house provision is to meet social needs and achieve the council's corporate objectives and priorities. The first priority of private firms is to ensure profitability for shareholders and to meet the demands of the marketplace.

Retaining and enhancing a public service ethos and values: In-house service delivery enables a public body to retain and enhance a public service ethos.

Ownership of assets: It should be the rule, not the exception, that public assets such as land, buildings, vehicles and equipment be retained within the public sector (unless there are compelling reasons based on community well-being criteria, or as a part of a strategy to secure the longer term future of public services, for their sale to the private or voluntary sector at full market value).

Sustainable development and sustainable communities: The achievement of sustainability objectives requires the vertical and horizontal integration of local and regional economic development policies and their implementation. This includes maximising the direct and indirect benefits from building and consolidating local and regional production and supply chains and minimising negative impacts on the environment. The alignment of strategic policy and implementation can only be fully achieved by direct provision.

Locally differentiated policies: Local strategies should be designed to meet the specific economic and social needs of the town, city and sub-region, not replaced by a national 'one size fits all' defined by market forces.

Mediation between internationalisation of the economy and neoliberal policies and addressing local needs and priorities: Local economic development strategies and policies, in effect, mediate between the continued internationalisation of the economy and specific local economic needs, which are required to enhance the local economy and community well-being. Local authorities need to retain flexibility and not be constrained by long-term contracts.

Democratic accountability

Direct democratic control and accountability of service delivery: In-house services are directly accountable to elected representatives. Outsourcing imposes contractual relations between a public body and a private contractor, thus reducing direct democratic control and community influence.

Participation of users/community organisations: Few public, private or voluntary organisations have a strong track record in engaging user and community organisations in substantive and meaningful participation on a continuous basis in the policy-making process. However, the public sector's record is superior, and avoids duplication of participation structures and processes between the public sector and contractor-led consultation.

Differentiating partnerships: It is important to differentiate between political and policy-driven partnerships, which are essentially organisational coalitions and alliances, and service delivery partnerships which are, in all but name, contracts subject to the procurement regulations and thus constrained by the inherent limitations of contracting.

Equalities and social justice

Addressing inequalities: The public sector is more committed to tackling inequalities and social exclusion.

Service provision: The public sector is more committed to improving access, participation in the planning and design of services, and to taking mitigating action to eliminate or reduce adverse impact.

Employment: The public sector's track record in addressing equalities and diversity in their workforce varies between authorities and services. However, it is exemplary compared to that of most private contractors and consultants.

Sustainable development

Local and regional supply chains: In-house providers are committed to creating and maintaining local and regional supply chains which support the local economy.

Protection of the environment and natural resources: In-house services have a better track record in preventing environmental damage and in taking initiatives to safeguard and enhance natural resources.

Improving public health: The health and safety record at work and in the community are central concerns of in-house services which operate to minimise pollution, improve standards of hygiene and cleanliness, control diseases, and improve community well-being.

Protecting the public interest

Minimising corruption: Procurement and commissioning (or the contracting system) can lead to 'collusion' between client officers and private firms who place the needs of the procurement system over social and community needs. Graft and corruption appear to have few boundaries, but the greater the involvement of private firms in the delivery of public services, the more likely there will be corruption and collusion, particularly as contracts get larger and longer-term.

Public Domain: Public provision has the advantage of taking a more holistic view by placing service delivery within a broader context and objectives. The intellectual knowledge accumulated by building the infrastructure, delivering local services, operating within social and political structures, and having an understanding of local needs, is retained within the public sector.

Financial advantages

Lower overall cost: A full cost comparison, which takes account of all client and commissioning costs, contract management, the cost of variation orders over the length of the contract (for additional work or changes to the contract) and other costs borne by the public sector, plus comparable employment costs, will usually demonstrate that in-house services can provide services at lower or equal cost. Budget holders often claim a 'saving', but this is usually absorbed by transaction costs borne by other departments or parts of the public sector. Where there is a mixed economy of provision, in-house services serve to regulate market prices.

Efficiency and effectiveness: At its best, public provision is equal to, or more, efficient and effective than private or voluntary sector provision. Chapter 3 described how efficiency is a means to an end, it is not an end itself. That is why it must always be discussed in connection with effectiveness and other objectives.

Economies of scale: Support services are more effectively delivered by in-house central services with economies of scale more equally shared between directorates and departments.

Avoidance of transaction costs: In-house provision avoids all the transaction costs incurred in the procurement and contracting process, which are additional to the cost of the service. They include the cost of advertising, consultants and advisers, preparation of contract documentation and contract management, which usually add between 3% and 5% to the cost.

Cost transparency: The true cost of in-house services can be more readily assessed than those of private or voluntary providers, who use commercial confidentiality to avoid disclosure. The full costs are usually obscured by the frequent use of the contract variation order system.

Corporate policies

Implementation of corporate policies and priorities: Policies on sustainable development, employment, social justice and community well-being are more effectively implemented directly through in-house services. The private sector's 'corporate social responsibility' falls well short of this and is more often in name only.

Coherence and fairness in support services: The range and quality of support services can be more fairly distributed between departments and services in a public authority compared with outsourcing scenarios.

Better quality employment

Quality of employment: The quality of service is best achieved when the quality of employment is also a key objective combining local government terms, conditions of service and pension scheme together with staff and trade union involvement in the planning and design of services, and an effective industrial relations framework. In-house services are less likely to use a high level of agency and temporary staff. A two-tier workforce is also much less likely to develop.

Training and workforce development: The vast bulk of training in core public services such as education, health and housing is provided by local and central government, the NHS and other public bodies. The level and quality of training and provision for staff education and learning is significantly better than that provided by private contractors.

Staff and trade union involvement in the planning, design and delivery of services: The public sector has a much better record than private contractors for continuing and sustainable involvement of frontline staff and trade unions in the planning, design and operation of service delivery.

Industrial relations framework: Comprehensive structures between employers and staff and trade unions in the public sector for policy making, employment, health and safety, and grievance procedures are an invaluable resource.

Trade union representation and organisation: Public sector workplaces have, on average, three times the level of membership compared to private sector workplaces. Studies have shown that trade union organised workplaces have higher wages and better terms and conditions compared to non-organised workplaces. Many private firms are hostile to trade unions and only adopt minimalist arrangements because they are required to do so under the European Union's Acquired Rights Directive.

Family friendly policies: Public sector employers, whilst not fully embracing the scope of family friendly policies, have a much better track record of implementation than the private sector, who often pay lip service unless it is in their economic interest to do otherwise.

Equalities and diversity: The commitment to, and implementation of, equality and diversity policies is on average more substantive in the public sector than with private contractors and consultants.

Capacity

Public sector intellectual capital: It is essential that public bodies retain ownership and control of the public sector's intellectual capital – the knowledge and information about the infrastructure, geography, and rationale of services and how they work. This vital information, built up over the years, is being freely transferred to the private sector through outsourcing of technical services and framework agreements.

Enhancing public sector capacity and skills: In-house provision helps to retain skills and experience which enables the authority to respond to changing demands and circumstances and to emergencies. It is also essential that public bodies retain the capacity to critically examine the potential impact of government, EU and business policies from a public service and local economy perspective.

Private sector ability frequently overstated: Public relations hype coupled with an ideological belief in the 'superiority' of private over public provision often leads to the private sector overstating its ability to deliver quality public services. The public sector knows best the complexity of services and community needs which it delivers through in-house provision.

CHAPTER 11

Strategies to oppose marketisation and support alternative policies

Since the process of marketisation consists of the interaction of a series of initiatives and policies, it is very easy to get drawn into relatively small-scale policy changes at the expense of the bigger picture. It is essential to maintain an overview. This section provides a summary of the action which can be taken to minimise the impact of marketisation and privatisation.

● Build political support
● Mobilise against
● Coalitions and alliances
● Intervene in modernisation process
● Promote alternative policies
● Prevent the extension of marketisation through the European Union and World Trade Organisation

Sustained and organised opposition to marketisation and privatisation must initially come from alliances and coalitions of local trade union and community organisations. Most local government organisations which opposed similar Tory policies in the 1990s are embedded in the Blairite agenda. National trade union opposition is tempered by constraining local activity arising from traditional control mechanisms and the unwritten part of the Warwick Agreement of not mobilising opposition to Labour's policies.

It is crucial that officers, managers and staff in public services be able to express their views and take action outside of the 'constraints' of their workplace. Similarly, many service users want to be able to express their views beyond the locality and discuss the implications and take action on a city-wide basis.

Build political support

● Critique government policy proposals and communicate them widely to members and other organisations and show how choice, personalisation and contestability will affect services, users and staff.
● Opposition to Strategic Service-delivery Partnerships and public private partnerships must be intensified since they have enormous impact on the accountability, quality, employment, organisation and

provision of public services, the social and physical infrastructure, and the regeneration process. Exposing the problems of private finance initiative/public private partnerships has little effect unless it is part of a wider organising and action strategy.

● Expose the longer-term consequences of the private finance initiative/public private partnership and a secondary market for the infrastructure and public services.

● Continue to research the design, quality, economics, cost, employment and refinancing of the private finance initiative/public private partnership.

● Advocate public service principles and values in the formulation of policies and implementation.

● Build public support for public service provision, good quality services and jobs through education, information, and use of the media.

● Challenge the policies and propaganda issued by trade associations and business organisations.

● Expose poor contract performance by private and voluntary organisations.

● Expose the failure of participatory and consultation 'exercises' to fully engage communities and staff.

● Expose the erosion of democratic accountability and transparency through 'commercial confidentiality' and the increased role of business in the public policy making process, leading to growth of a corporate welfare complex.

● Challenge business and vested interests and demand new controls over capital with re-regulation, rigorous monitoring, scrutiny and evaluation.

● Challenge the ability and community objectives of black and ethnic minority and women only businesses, social enterprises and voluntary organisations, and the exploitation of these organisations by the government to make its marketisation and privatisation policies more 'palatable'.

Mobilise against specific policies and projects

● Organise campaigns to oppose Academies, Foundation Hospitals and school trusts, and other proposals to transfer services and assets to arms length companies and trusts (the success of Conisbrough & District Parents Action Group in stopping the academy; the Camden tenants' successful campaign against an arms length management

organisation; planned leisure trusts stopped by UNISON branches in South Tyneside and Newcastle; Relatives' Action Group for the Elderly campaign to stop residential homes closures in Birmingham).
● Organise patient/user boycotts of private sector Treatment Centres and support and encourage users opting for public sector options.
● Draw on the tactics used by campaigns against Academies (see Socialist Teacher Alliance (www.socialist-teacher.org).
● Use selective industrial action in marketisation and privatisation campaigns.
● Research and expose vested interests of private contractors and business and trade organisations (see the Investigators Handbook, Centre for Public Services).

Organise coalitions and alliances

This should include organising the chain of production of public services, which will increasingly extend from in-house provision to home-working to voluntary organisations and the social economy, to local, national and/or international locations of private firms. More broad-based movements for economic and social justice beyond the workplace and workers' rights will be essential. Trade unions have a vital role in organising, representing, bargaining, educating, training, and monitoring in an era of increasing insecurity.
● Build coalitions and alliances between trade unions, community and civil society organisations, which promote public service and democratic values and challenge business values (Building Schools for the Future Tyne and Wear campaign combining teachers (NUT and NASUWT) and council unions (UNISON and GMB), with a charter of proposals and exclusion of support services; national network against Academies, established after Birmingham conference in October 2005 attended by fifteen campaigns).
● Organise, recruit and strengthen representation, particularly in those services likely to be targeted for review and procurement.
● Establish local/regional alliances of trade unions, community organisations, user organisations, tenants and civil society organisations in a wide coalition of interests to oppose marketisation and privatisation. Alliances could be initiated and supported by Public Service Alliances, Trades Councils or similar bodies.
● Build a national coalition of trade unions, public sector alliances, community and civil society organisations through regional and national action. This could start from several city-based

coalitions/alliances forging a wider network.

● Defend Council Housing is a good example of a successful national campaign based on national analysis and organising, Parliamentary lobbying, local campaigns, trade union and community support.

● Campaign for a Trade Union Freedom Bill which would include the abolition of restrictive balloting, the right to strike, freedom to take solidarity action for workers who are in dispute, and strengthened protection against exploitation and discrimination of migrant, agency and temporary workers and ethnic minorities.

Intervene in the modernisation process

● Prepare critiques of options appraisals and outline business cases on the basis that they have not established need, excluded or dismissed public sector options, failed to assess the impact on the local economy, have not addressed equalities and sustainable development, made unsubstantiated claims about the capacity and experience of the private sector, ignored secondment employment models, and assumed TUPE provides full security.

● Make the case for the exclusion of support services from the private finance initiative/public private partnership projects (Newcastle UNISON and in-house teams succeeded in excluding facilities management and information and communications technology services from Newcastle City Council's £140m Building Schools for the Future project).

● Research and challenge the local and regional content of private contractors' production and supply chains.

● Organise and recruit the staff of private contractors supplying public services.

● Demand that Scrutiny Committees investigate the performance of contracts and partnerships, procurement policies and projects using integrated impact assessment to identify the full effects on services, jobs, economies and communities.

● Intervene in the procurement and commissioning processes:
  – Make a detailed case against strategic partnerships and outsourcing (Salford City Council decided against starting procurement and Kent County Council, Northamptonshire County Council, Walsall MBC and Dacorum Borough Council decided to adopt an in-house strategy during the procurement process).

– Demand that in-house bids and public sector consortia options are fully developed and fairly assessed (Newcastle UNISON's two year campaign resulted in submission of a successful in-house bid for a £200m strategic partnership won against BT).

– Ensure the preparation of in-house bids are fully supported and resourced.

– Ensure that Procurement Policy protocols set out trade union and community involvement in the options appraisal and procurement processes together with involvement in the scoping, short-listing, specification and evaluation stages.

– Community benefits such as increased employment, training, community facilities, and affordable housing should be identified for all major procurements.

– Comprehensive evaluation criteria including sustainable development, community well-being, corporate impact, social justice and equalities should be used for the appraisal, selection and bid evaluation stages.

● Demand that all policies and projects should be subjected to a social justice impact assessment at both the planning and post-implementation stages.

● Ensure service and efficiency reviews fully engage frontline staff and users in a comprehensive review and scrutiny process.

● Maximise employment protection particularly by advocating the secondment model and pensions protection.

● Demand re-regulation of markets and private companies.

● Build in-house capacity and retention of public sector intellectual capital by minimising use of consultants; capacity building should be a contractual requirement of all framework agreements.

● Maintain a high level of trade union organisation and representation in arms length companies and trusts and make the case for their transfer back to public sector direct control.

Promote alternative policies

● Develop and promote alternative policies and strategies (summary on page 138).

● Make the case for in-house provision, bids and options, public sector consortia models and public investment.

● Demonstrate that there are alternative ways and existing best practice of increasing choice, freedom and flexibility within the public sector.

Action against European Union
and World Trade Organisation liberalisation plans

● Monitor the drafting of the revised European Union Services Directive and, if necessary, take further action if the Council of Ministers and national interpretation of the Directive weakens previous agreements.

● Lobby and support the campaign against the General Agreement for Trade in Services currently being negotiated by the World Trade Organisation.

● Persuade public bodies to support the GATS-free-zones campaign and to link up with similar campaigns across Europe.

● Non-Governmental Organisations such as the World Development Movement, Oxfam and War on Want should link their opposition to Britain's position on the European Internal Market for Services and World Trade Organisation GATS negotiations to oppose Britain's internal marketisation and privatisation programme.

● Work with unions internationally in a direct and practical way.

● Hold joint education and training sessions for members to develop a better understanding of government and European Union policies and the most effective strategies.

CHAPTER 12

Lessons for Europe

Marketisation and privatisation is more advanced in Britain than any other European country. The precise application of these policies will vary between countries for political, legal and cultural reasons. Nonetheless, there are key lessons from the experience in Britain which should be drawn upon.

This chapter has three elements – summarising the lessons learnt from marketisation, from public private partnerships, and from action strategies.

Marketisation process
● Marketisation may start with individual services such as information and communication technology, transport and 'back office' services but will affect all services including health, education, social care and criminal justice.
● The state and capital will combine to produce half-truths and construct 'research' findings comparing public and private sector performance using selective 'evidence' and 'survey findings'.
● Importance of monitoring, scrutinising and evaluating contracts and projects.
● Need to shift the narrow evaluation agenda away from financial, efficiency, risk transfer and value for money criteria to an integrated impact assessment covering social, economic, equalities, sustainable development and community well-being assessment.
● Public money will be diverted from frontline provision and squandered on an army of consultants and transaction costs.
● The formation of arms length companies and trusts will inevitably result in them demanding freedom and flexibility via newly established trade associations to represent their vested interests.
● Financial and business interests will want secondary markets to be established to secure additional sources of profit and to further financialise and valorise public service provision.
● Applying the 'corporate citizen' concept to the public sector is naïve and will be exploited by business interests to further increase corporate power and the corporate welfare complex whilst minimising private sector contribution to sustainable development.
● Projects and programmes will get ever more technically,

organisationally and financially complex which will stretch the capacity of public organisations (leading to further outsourcing to consultants), making political understanding and control very difficult, and thus reinforcing the trend towards managerialism.

● Demand meaningful choice within public services where this is integral to the quality of service and can be achieved without undue costs and negative impacts.

Public Private Partnerships

● Public private partnership infrastructure projects may initially focus on individual buildings and facilities management but will eventually extend to area-wide provision and core public services.

● The rationale for public private partnerships in terms of no alternative finance, value for money, efficiency, risk transfer and private sector vision and innovation has never been proven in Britain.

● Alternative in-house proposals or bids, focusing on service improvements and harnessing in-house resources and expertise, have succeeded in stopping public private partnerships in several local authorities.

● The exclusion of services or successful in-house bids for services such as ICT and facilities management can significantly reduce the scope of public private partnerships.

● The secondment rather than the transfer of staff in several public private partnerships has helped to maintain public sector terms and conditions and avoided a two-tier workforce.

● Governments will establish quangos to drive the public private partnerships and marketisation agenda to try to coerce local and regional public sector bodies to participate.

● National or local social partnerships should not be entered into if they require the support of public private partnerships and marketisation.

Action strategies

● All public sector workers – support, administration and professional – are likely to be affected sooner rather then later.

● Coalitions, alliances and joint trade union and community campaigns are essential to unite opposition and build political support.

● Public private partnerships cannot be stopped or substantially changed through research or intellectual arguments about economics or value for money alone. They are propelled by ideology and long-term business interests, which requires organising and mobilising political opposition at local, regional, national, and European levels.

● Always demand the submission of in-house bids.

● Challenge the erosion of values and weakening application of public service principles.

● Constantly challenge the private sector's claims of efficiency and value for money by exposing the lack of evidence.

● Politicise all procurement processes by making sure elected members, the media and the public are made aware of the key issues at each stage of the process.

● Never assume a contract or project cannot be stopped or terminated.

● Intervention strategies designed to promote in-house bids, exclude support services, minimise staff transfer, and ensure evaluation based on community well-being and sustainable development criteria can be highly successful when they combine organising and political action with technical know-how.

● Analysis of the impact of marketisation and privatisation policies, projects and programmes must be made swiftly with strategic advice and support provided to trade union branches so that they respond at the formative stages.

● Information on companies and consultants' performance, corporate track records, and conflicts of interest is vitally important but rarely stops the procurement process or a contract award.

Glossary

Asset Based Welfare State: Increasing the role of property, personal savings, insurance and other financial mechanisms to help to fund welfare services. Associated with individual rather than collective responsibility.

Back-office services: Services such as transactional and financial services, human resources, property management, legal services.

Barriers to entry: The ease with which private firms can gain access to or exit a market. Barriers could include the cost, regulatory frameworks, and/or size of contracts.

Business Plan: A plan setting out how an organisation will operate, invest and improve in the future, usually a three-year period.

Cashable / Non-Cashable: Cashable efficiency gains include those where cash savings have been realised, or input costs have been decreased, releasing cash. Increased input levels (e.g. through reduced absenteeism) or increased output levels represent non-cashable efficiency gains.

Cherry picking: Treating low cost cases or those which are the most profitable, selecting tasks which can be completed quickly or easily,

Choice: Having the option of more than one provider of a service.

Client/contractor: The functional and managerial separation of responsibilities in an organisation between those commissioning or purchasing services and those responsible for delivering the service (see purchaser/provider).

Commercialisation: The process by which local authority and public sector organisations adopt private sector values and organisational structures.

Commodification: The process of designing and packaging services so that they can be delivered by external providers. Usually includes identifying utilisation of assets and support services, ring-fencing of funding, reviewing standards and working practices.

Commissioning: The term has traditionally been used to describe a decision to appoint architects to design a building or to engage consultants. It is also used at a strategic level, for example by the NHS commissioning services from NHS Trusts. In social care it is used to describe the delivery of services at the individual, community or local authority levels. The Audit Commission, the

Social Services Inspectorate and the National Assembly of Wales have jointly defined social care commissioning as: having the vision and commitment to improve services; connecting with the needs and aspirations of users and carers; making the best use of all available resources; understanding demand and supply; linking financial planning and service planning, and making relationships and working in partnerships.

Competitive sourcing: Another name for competitive tendering and commonly used in the United States.

Competitive tendering: The process by which public services are required to compete with the private sector through the procurement process.

Contestability: 'Contestability' is achieved by the threat of other providers entering the market, thus putting pressure on the existing provider to maintain quality and efficient services. It also requires that there are no significant barriers to the entry or exit of other providers.

Contract condition: The rules governing the operation of a contract which sets out the legal responsibilities of both client and contractor.

Contract management: A client responsibility covering how the authority monitors and enforces the contract and relations with the contractor.

Contracting out: Contracting out is another term for outsourcing. Services or functions (and staff) are transferred to a private contractor or voluntary organisation for a specific period.

Community benefit: Employment, training and social benefits provided by a contractor in the delivery of services or capital works.

Corporate welfare complex: A system which prioritises the interests of contractors, consultants and business associations.

Corporate citizen: The idea that a company should be treated as a citizen with rights and responsibilities.

Corporate Social Responsibility: The social, community and environmental responsibilities that some companies have to guide investment and activities.

Cream skimming: see cherry picking.

Deregulation: The relaxation or elimination of regulations to allow business greater freedom to operate in service and labour markets.

Efficiency: The Gershon Review defined 'efficiencies' as being achieved by five types of reform to delivery processes and resources (including workforce). Efficiency in the context of Productive Time is defined as: producing more output for the same input cost and with the same or greater quality, or producing the same output at lower input cost and with the same or greater quality.

Enabling: The state funds and facilitates the private and voluntary sectors to deliver services and perform public functions. Government only directly provides services as a last resort.

Externalisation: The transfer or trade sale of Direct Service Organisations or business units from the public to the private sector.

Evaluation: The process by which proposals and bids are assessed including financial, technical, employment, management and corporate assessment.

Front-line staff: Staff who serve an organisation's aims directly, usually through regular, direct contact with the people for whom the service is provided, by undertaking core activities.

Fully open: creating conditions to allow new entrants into a competitive market for public services.

Gaming: Tactics used by service providers to avoid or minimise delivering services to users who require a high level of resources, time and/or specialist support. See also parking.

Gateway Review: An Office of Government Commerce process for best-practice procurement and project evaluation.

Gershon Review: A review of ways of increasing public sector efficiency carried out for HM Treasury by Sir Peter Gershon and published with the 2004 Spending Review in July 2004.

Green procurement: Another way of describing sustainable procurement.

In-house bid: A bid to provide a service prepared by the in-house service or direct service organisation.

Liberalisation: Usually a mixture of deregulation and new regulatory frameworks to create more open and accessible goods and services markets.

Loss leader: Submitting a low bid in order to win contracts and gain/sustain market share; contractor usually tries to recoup earlier losses later in contract.

Managed services: The delivery of a group or package of services, usually corporate services, by a single contractor.

Marketisation: The process of preparing public services so that they can be packaged and priced into a contract and open to competitive tendering. The process may also include establishing regulations, subsidies and other mechanisms to encourage the development of market conditions.

Offshoring: Offshoring is the combination of outsourcing and transfer of services and functions overseas, usually to Asia.

Options appraisal: The assessment of the effects of options and selection of the option, which is most effective and efficient in meeting objectives and priorities.

Outsourcing: Outsourcing is another term for 'contracting out'. Services or functions (and staff) are transferred to a private contractor or voluntary organisation for a specific period.

Parking: The non-treatment of clients who are harder to help, leaving difficult and complex (and therefore costly) cases for the public sector or another contractor. For example, in employment training targeting those with aptitude and basic skills and 'parking' those without to another training programme.

Personalisation: The new term used for the design and funding of services built around the needs of individuals.

Preferred bidder: Selection of a provisional contractor, which will be followed by detailed negotiations on service delivery, employment and prices.

Prime contractor: A single contractor who acts as the sole point of responsibility to a public sector client for the management and delivery of a project. Widely used in construction industry.

Privatisation: The sales of assets or transfer of services and functions from the public to the private sector.

Procurement: '... the process for acquiring goods, works and services, covering both acquisition from third parties and from in-house providers. The process spans the whole cycle from identification of need, through to the end of a service contract or the end of the useful life of an asset. It involves options appraisal and the critical 'make or buy' decisions, which may result in the provision of in-house services in appropriate circumstances.' (National Procurement Strategy, Local Government Association, 2003)

Productive time: Time spent by public service professionals on core activities.

Productivity: Commonly defined as a ratio of a volume measure of output to a volume measure of input.

Purchaser/provider split: The functional and managerial separation of responsibilities in an organisation between those commissioning or purchasing services and those responsible for delivering the service (see client/contractor).

Public service agreement (PSA): An agreement between a government department and the Treasury, as part of the Spending Review, including objectives and targets.

Risk transfer: The identification and pricing of risk and its transfer from the public to the private sector.

Secondary market: An additional market to the initial private financing of private finance initiative and public private partnership projects in which projects are refinanced and equity stakes in projects are resold.

Shared services: Joint provision of corporate services such as information and communication technology, financial and human resources between two or more public bodies.

Social enterprise: A business with primarily social objectives whose surpluses are principally reinvested for that purpose in the business or in the community.

Soft services: Cleaning, catering, routine repairs and maintenance, security and similar support services which are considered separate from the 'hard' services which are directly connected to the building fabric.

Specification: A description of the work, quality, standards and inputs, outputs, outcomes and processes required in the delivery of a service.

Strategic service-delivery partnerships (SSPs): These are long-term, multi-service, multi-million pound contracts involving the secondment or transfer of between 100 – 1000 staff to a private contractor. Usually include information and communications technology, human resources, financial, property management and other corporate services.

Subcontracting: When a contractor engages another contractor to undertake part of the contract.

Supply chain: Suppliers and sub-contractors involved in the supply and transport of materials, goods, services and equipment during the construction and operation of the building and services.

Supplier: An organisation or company delivering goods, services and works.

Sustainable procurement: Procurement which takes maximum account of environmental and sustainable development factors.

Tendering: Tendering is the 'old' term used to describe the contracting process which usually began with the selection of services to be tendered, specification and contract documents through to contract award. The system remains largely the same. Commissioning and procurement encompass the earlier stages of planning, needs analysis, service review and options appraisal.

Transaction costs: The costs incurred in the process of planning, contracting and procuring goods and services including the cost of advertising contracts, engaging consultants, officer time in preparing contract documentation, and client costs of managing and monitoring the contract.

Value for money: The optimum combination of whole life cost and quality to meet the users requirements.

Weighting: A means of expressing the prioritising criteria by allocating different numerical values to each criterion.

Whole-life costing: Assessing the total costs of a building or project over a contract period taking account of responsive repairs and maintenance, planned maintenance, and renewal/replacement cycles.

References

Ackerman, F. (2005) *The Shrinking Gains from Trade: A Critical Assessment of Doha Round Projections*, Working Paper No 05-01, Global Development and Environment Institute, Tufts University, Boston.

Appleby, J., Harrison, A. and Delvin, N. (2003) *What is the Real Cost of More Patient Choice?*, King's Fund, London.

Audit Commission (2005) *CPA – The harder test*, June, London.

Audit Commission (2005) Early *Lessons from Payment by Results*, October, London.

Audit Commission (2006) *The Planning System: Matching Expectations and Capacity*, February, London.

Banks, P. (2005) *Commissioning Care Services for Older People*, King's Fund, June, London.

Brenner, N. and Theodore, N. (2002) *Spaces of Neoliberalism: Urban Restructuring in North America and Western Europe*, Blackwell, Oxford.

Bristol North PCT (2003) *The Evercare Programme: Summary*, Bristol.

British Medical Association (2005) *Health Policy Review*, Vol 1, Issue 1, The Future Direction of the NHS, London.

British Property Federation, Investment Property Forum and Royal Institution of Chartered Surveyors (2005), *UK Real Estate Investment Trusts – A Response from the BPF, IPF and RICS*, May, London.

Building (2005) DfES pledges to cut bid costs of schools for future, 13 December.

Burgess, S. Propper, C. and Wilson, D. (2005) *Choice: Will More Choice Improve Outcomes in Education and Health Care? The Evidence of Economic Research*, Centre for Market and Public Organisation, University of Bristol.

Butcher, J. (2005) Government, *The Third Sector and the Rise of Social Capital*, Centre for Research in Public Sector Management, October, University of Canberra, Canberra.

Cabinet Office and Department of Health (2005) *Making A Difference: Direct Payments*, April, London.

Centre for International Public Health Policy (2005) Briefing Note for the House of Commons Public Accounts Committee on the National Audit Office report: *Innovation in the NHS: Local Improvement Finance Trusts*, University of Edinburgh, Edinburgh.

Centre for Public Services (2001) *Private Finance Initiative and Public Private Partnerships: What Future for Public Services?*, www.centre.public.org.uk

Centre for Public Services (2003) *The Investigator's Handbook: A guide to investigating companies, organisations, government and individuals*, February, Sheffield.

Centre for Public Services (2003) *Mortgaging Our Children's Future*, June, Sheffield.

Centre for Public Services (2004) *The Case for the 4th Option for Council Housing: and a Critique of Arms Length Management Organisations*, May, Sheffield.

Centre for Public Services (2004) *How to Exclude Support Services from BSF and PFI/PPP Projects, A Best Practice Report for UNISON, GMB, NUT and NASUWT in Tyne and Wear using HM Treasury VfM Methodolgy*, December, Sheffield.

Centre for Public Services (2005) *Strategic Partnership in Crisis*, Bedfordshire UNISON, March, Sheffield.

Centre for Public Services (2005) *Secondment of Staff for the New Tyne Tunnel, Newcastle UNISON.*

Centre for Public Services (2006) *Outsourcing and PPP* Library www.centre.public.org.uk/outsourcing.

Chang, Ha-Joon (2001) *Breaking the Mould: An Institutionalist Political Economy Alternative to the Neoliberal Theory of the Market and the State*, United Nations Research Institute for Social Development, Programme Paper No 6,

Citizens Network on Essential Services (2005) *Public Services at Risk: GATS and the privatisation agenda*, Canada.

Cohen, A. (2004) *Practice Based Commissioning in the NHS: The Implications for Mental Health*, The Sainsbury Centre for Mental Health, London.

Confederation of British Industry (2004) *Delivering for Local Government: The Impact of Public-Private Partnerships*, London.

Confederation of British Industry (2005) *The Business of Education Improvement*, January, London.

Confederation of British Industry (2006) *A Fair Field and No Favours: Competitive Neutrality in UK Public Service Markets*, January, London.

Confederation of British Industry (2006) *Children First: The Power of Choice in Children's Services*, January, London.

Corlyon, J. and Meadows, P. (2004) Methods Paper: *Defining a Local Childcare Market*, Tavistock Institute for Human Relations and

National Institute of Economic and Social Research, April, DfES, London.

Crime and Society Foundation (forthcoming) *Why Who Delivers Matters: Critical Perspectives on Contestability and Marketisation*, Kings College, London.

Curtis, M. (2005) *17 Ways the European Commission is Pushing Trade Liberalisation on Poor Countries*, Christian Aid, London.

DfES (2004) *Five Year Strategy for Children and Learners*, July, London.

DfES (2004) *Scoping the market for children's services*, Pricewaterhouse Coopers, October, London.

DfES (2005) *Academies Sponsors Prospectus* – www.standards.dfes.gov.uk/academies

DfES and PartnershipsUK (2005) *Schools PFI – Post-Signature Review*, Phase 2 Report, May, London.

DfES (2005) *Academies Evaluation: 2nd Annual Report*, PriceWaterhouse Coopers, London.

DfES (2005) *Higher Standards, Better Schools for All: More choice for parents and pupils*, Cm 6677, October, London.

Department of Health (2004) *The NHS Improvement Plan: Putting People at the Heart of Public Services*, June, London.

Department of Health (2004) *Reconfiguring the Department of Health's Arm's Length Bodies*, July, London.

Department of Health (2004) *An Implementation Framework for Reconfiguring the Department of Health's Arm's Length Bodies: Redistributing resources to the NHS frontline*, November, London.

Department of Health (2005) *Creating a Patient-Led NHS: Delivering the NHS Improvement Plan*, March, London.

Department of Health (2005) *Treatment Centres: Delivering Faster, Quality care and Choice for NHS Patients*, January, London.

Department of Health (2005) *Independence, Well-being and Choice: Our vision for the future of social care for adults in England*, Green Paper, Cm 6499, March, London.

Department of Health (2005) *Government Response to the Office of Fair Trading (OFT) Care Homes Study*, August, London.

Department of Health (2005) *Payment by Results and the Market Forces Factor*, London.

Department of Health (2005) *Code of Conduct for Payment by Results*: Draft for Consultation, August, London.

Department of Health (2005) *Practice Based Commissioning: Engaging Practices in Commissioning*, October, London.

Department of Health (2005) *Health Reform in England: update and next steps*, December, London.

Department of Health (2006) *Our Health, Our Care, Our Say: A New Direction for Community Services*, Cm 6737, January, London.

Department of Health (2006) *Independent Sector Treatment Centres, Report from Commercial Director*, February, London.

Department of Trade and Industry (2002) *Liberalising Trade in Services: A new consultation on the World Trade Organisation's GATS negotiations*, London.

Department of Trade (2004) *EU Directive on Services in the Internal Market: Consultation Document*, March, London.

Department of Trade and Industry (2005) *Public Policy: Using Market Based Approaches, Lessons and Guidance for Policy Makers*, September, London.

Department of Work and Pensions (2006) *A New Deal for Welfare: Empowering People into Work*, Cm 6730, January, London.

Economic and Social Research Council (2006) *Creating Citizen-Consumers: Changing Relationships and Identifications*, Prof John Clarke, Open University, Milton Keynes.

Farnsworth, K. (2004) *Corporate Power and Social Policy in a Global Economy: British Welfare Under the Influence*, The Policy Press, Bristol.

Ferrand, D., Gibson, A. and Scott, H. (2004) *Making Markets Work for the Poor: An Objective and An Approach for Governments and Development Agencies*, ComMark Trust, July, Woodmead, South Africa.

Florio, M. (2004) *The Great Divestiture*, MIT Press, Cambridge, Mass.

Foundation Trust Network (2005) *Foundation Trusts: Future Thinking, Challenges and Change*, London.

Foundation Trust Network (2005) *Opportunities for Developing the Business*, Conference Overview, London.

Gough, J. (2002) 'Neoliberalism and Socialisation in the Contemporary City: Opposites, Complements and Instabilities', in Brenner and Theodore, *Spaces of Neoliberalism: Urban Restructuring in North America and Western Europe*, Blackwell, Oxford.

Hall, D., Lobina, M. and de la Motte, R. (2005) 'Public Resistance to Privatisation in Water and Energy', *Development in Practice*, Vol. 15, Numbers 3 and 4, June.

Health Service Journal (2005) 'Independent Treatment Centres: What Chief Executives Really Think', 20 January.

Hewitt, MP, Patricia, (2005) 'Investment and Reform: Transforming

Health and Healthcare': Annual Health and Social Care Lecture, London School of Economics, 13 December, London.

Higher Education Funding Council for England (2005) *Strategically Important and Vulnerable Subjects*, Report of Advisory Group, Paper 2005/24, London.

HM Treasury (2004a) *Releasing Resources to the Frontline: Independent Review of Public Sector Efficiency*, Sir Peter Gershon, July, London.

HM Treasury (2004b) *Spending Review 2004*, July, London.

HM Treasury and Cabinet Office (2004) *Devolving Decision Making: 1 – Delivering better public services: refining targets and performance management*, March, London.

HM Treasury (2005) *Securing Better Outcomes: Developing a new performance framework*, January, London.

HM Treasury and Inland Revenue (2005) *UK Real Estate Investment Trusts: A Discussion Paper*, March, London.

HM Treasury and Office of Deputy Prime Minister (2005) *The Government's Response to Kate Barker's Review of Housing Supply*, London.

Home Office (2004) *Enhancing the Role of the Voluntary and Community Sector: A Case study of the Yorkshire and Humber Region*, National Offender Management Service, London.

Home Office (2005) *Together We Can: People and Government, Working Together to Make Life Better*, Civil Renewal Unit, London.

House of Commons Education and Skills Select Committee (2005) *Secondary Education, Fifth Report of Session 2004/05*, March, London.

House of Commons Education and Skills Select Committee (2006) *The Schools White Paper: Higher Standards, Better Schools for All*, HC 633, January, London.

House of Commons Public Administration Select Committee (2005) *Choice, Voice and Public Services*, March, London.

House of Commons Trade and Industry Committee (2005) *Royal Mail After Liberalisation, Second Report of Session 2005-06, Vol 1, HC 570-1*, December, London.

House of Commons Library (2005) *Employment and Training Programmes for the Unemployed: Vol 1: recent developments and the New Deal programmes*, Research Paper 05/61, September, London.

House of Commons (2004) *The Case for User Choice in Public Services, Public Administration Select Committee Inquiry into Choice, Voice and Public Services*: Joint Memorandum From Minister For State For Department Of Health; Minister of State for Local and Regional Government; and Minister of State for School Standards, London.

House of Commons Committee of Public Accounts (2005) *PFI: The STEPS Deal*, April, London.

HouseMark (2005) HouseMark ALMO Performance Improvement Club: Quarterly Performance Indicator Tracking, 2004/5 Year End Results, August. www.housemark.co.uk

Select Committee, *Fourth Report of Session 2004–05, Volume I*, London.

Improvement & Development Agency and Local Government Association (2004) *Local Public Service Boards*, July, London.

Inside Housing (2005) 'Appraisals fuel doubts over decent homes target', 5 August.

Inside Housing (2005) 'Association invests £2m in schools academy scheme', 2 December.

Institute for Public Policy Research (2005) *The Future of Public Services Regulation*, December, London.

International Monetary Fund (2004) *Public Private Partnerships*, Washington DC.

Jessop, B. (2002) 'Liberalism, Neoliberalism and Urban Governance: A State-Theoretical Perspective', in Brenner and Theodore, *Spaces of Neoliberalism: Urban Restructuring in North America and Western Europe*, Blackwell, Oxford.

Kaul, I., Conceicao, P, Le Goulven, K. and Mendoza, R. (2003) *Providing Global Public Goods*, Oxford University Press, Oxford.

Kings Fund (2005) *Understanding Public Services and Care Markets*, Care Services Inquiry, June, London.

Kings Fund (2005) *The Business of Caring*, June, London.

KPMG and Business Services Association (2005) *Effectiveness of Operational Contracts in PFI*, London.

Laing and Buisson (2005) *Children's Nurseries 2005*, London.

Lewis, R. and Dixon, J. (2005) *NHS Market Futures: Exploring the impact of health service market reforms*, Kings Fund, June, London.

Leys, Colin. (2001) *Market-Driven Politics: Neo-liberal Democracy and the Public Interest*, Verso, London.

Local Government Association (2004) *Independence, Opportunity, Trust: A Manifesto for Local Communities*, September, London.

Management Consultancies Association (2005) *The UK Consultancy Industry 2004/5*, London.

McCreevy, C. (2005) Statement to the European Parliament on Services Directive, European Commissioner for Internal Market and Services, European Parliament Plenary Session, 8 March, Strasbourg.

Milburn, A. (2004) 'The Future of Public Private Partnerships', PPP Forum Conference, 1 July, Birmingham.

Milios, J. (2005) 'European Integration as a Vehicle of Neoliberal Hegemony', in Saad-Filho and Johnstone, *Neoliberalism: A Critical Reader*, Pluto Press, London.

Minister of State for Department of Health, Minister of State for Local and Regional Government and Minister of State for School Standards (2004) 'The Case for User Choice in Public Services: Joint Memorandum', Public Administration Select Committee Inquiry into Choice, Voice and Public Services, London.

Ministry of Defence (2005) 'Review of MoD PFI Projects in Construction and Operation', Ministry of Defence PFI Unit, December, London.

Munck, R. (2005) 'Neoliberalism and Politics, and the Politics of Neoliberalism', in Saad-Filho and Johnstone, *Neoliberalism: A Critical Reader*, Pluto Press, London.

National Audit Office (2000) Refinancing the Fazakerly PFI Prison Contract, HC 584, June, London.

National Audit Office (2002) PFI Refinancing Update, HC 1288, November, London.

National Audit Office (2004) Refinancing the Public Private Partnership for the National Air Traffic Services, HC 157, January, London.

National Audit Office (2004) PFI: The STEPS Deal, HC 530, Session 2003/04, May, London.

National Audit Office (2005) The Refinancing of the Norfolk and Norwich PFI Hospital: How the deal can be viewed in the light of refinancing, June, London.

National Audit Office (2005) Patient Choice at the Point of GP Referral, HC 180, Session 2004-05, January, London.

National Centre for Health Outcomes Development (2005) ISTC Performance Management Analysis Service, Preliminary Overview Report for GSU1C, OC123, LP4 and LP5, October, London.

National Centre for Social Research (2004) *Childcare: How Local Markets Respond to National Initiatives*, April, London.

National Centre for Social Research (2005) *Local Childcare Markets – A Longitudinal Study*, for DfES and Inland Revenue, June, London.

National Centre for Vocational Education Research (2005) *Trading Places: The Impact and Outcomes of Market reforms in Vocational Education and Training*, Adelaide.

National Offender Management Service (2005) *Partial Regulatory Impact Assessment: Restructuring Probation to Reduce Re-Offending*, November, London.

National Offender Management Service (2005) *Strategic Business Case*, London.

National Offender Management Service (2005) *The NOMS Offender Management Model*, London.

National Union of Teachers (2006) *Academies Briefing*, London (www.teachers.org.uk).

Office of the Deputy Prime Minister (2004) The Future of Local Government: Developing a 10 year Vision, June, London.

Office of the Deputy Prime Minister (2004) Guidance on the Business Improvement Districts (England) Regulations 2004, London.

Office of the Deputy Prime Minister (2005a) 'Meta-evaluation of the Local Government Modernisation Agenda: Progress Report on Service Improvement in Local Government', Steve Martin and Tony Bovaird, Centre for Local & Regional Government Research, Cardiff University and Bristol Business School, University of the West of England, March, London.

Office of the Deputy Prime Minister (2005b) *Citizen Engagement, Neighbourhoods and Public Services: Evidence from Local Government*, January, London.

Office of the Deputy Prime Minister (2005) *Sustainable Communities, People, Places and Prosperity: A Five Year Plan from the Office of the Deputy Prime Minister*, Cm 6425, January, London.

Office of the Deputy Prime Minister and Housing Corporation (2005) Management Statement and Financial Memorandum for the Housing Corporation, April, London.

Office of the Deputy Prime Minister (2005) *Vibrant Local Leadership*, January, London.

Office of the Deputy Prime Minister (2005) *Citizen Engagement and Public Services: Why Neighbourhoods Matter*, January, London.

Office of the Deputy Prime Minister (2005) *New Localism – Citizen Engagement, Neighbourhood and Public Services*, January, London.

Office of Government Commerce (2003) *Increasing Competition and Improving Long-Term Capacity Planning in the Government Market Place*, Report to the Exchequer, December, London.

Office of Public Service Reform (2002) *Reforming Our Public Services: Principles into Practice*, Cabinet Office, London.

Organisation for Economic Co-operation and Development (2004)

Services Trade Liberalisation: Identifying Opportunities and Gains, Trade Policy Working Paper No 1, Julia Nelson and Daria Taglioni, Paris.

Organisation for Economic Co-operation and Development (2005) *Growth in Services: Fostering Employment, Productivity and Innovation*, Meeting of OECD Council at Ministerial Level, May.

Organisation for Economic Co-operation and Development (2005) *The Service Economy in OECD Countries*, STI Working Paper 2005/3, Anita Wolfl, Paris.

Organisation for Economic Co-operation and Development (2005) *The European Union's Single Market: At Your Service?* Economics Department Working Paper No 449, October, Paris.

Organisation for Economic Co-operation and Development (2005) *Economic Survey of the Euro Area 2005*, Paris.

Organisation for Economic Co-operation and Development (2005) *Public Sector Modernisation: The Way Forward*, Policy Brief, November, Paris.

Palley, T. (2005) 'From Keynesianism to Neoliberalism: Shifting Paradigms in Economics', in Saad-Filho and Johnstone, *Neoliberalism: A Critical Reader*, Pluto Press, London.

Palmer, K. (2005) *How Should We Deal With Hospital Failure?*, King's Fund, London.

Pannggabean, A. (2005) *Using Market Mechanisms to Expand Access to Basic Services in Asia: Public-Private Partnerships for Poverty Reduction* (draft), Asian Development Bank, February.

Partnerships for Schools (2004) *The Local Education Partnership Model*, London.

Pinter, Harold (2005) 'Pinter v the US, Nobel acceptance speech', *The Guardian*, 8 December.

Pollock, A. (2004) *NHS plc: The Privatisation of our Health Care*, Verso, London.

Postal Services Commission (2004) *Postcomm and Postal Services*, London.

Postal Services Commission (2005) *Tackling Barriers to Entry in Postal Services*, March, London.

Postal Services Commission (2005) 'Postcomm to do more to encourage competition', June, London.

PriceWaterhouseCoopers (2005) *Delivering the PPP Promise: A review of PPP issues and activity*, London.

Reform (2005) *The NHS in 2010: Reform or Bust*, London.

Saad-Filho, A and Johnstone, D. (2005) *Neoliberalism: A Critical Reader*,

Pluto Press, London.

Shafaeddin, S.M. (2004) *Who is the Master? Who is the Servant? Market or Government? An alternative approach: Towards a coordination system*, United Nations Conference on Trade and Development, Discussion Paper, No. 175, August, Geneva.

Shirley, M. and Walsh, P (2002) *Public verses Private Ownership: The Current State of the Debate*, World Bank, Washington.

Sinclair, S. (2005) The GATS, *South African Local Governments and Water Services*, Canadian Centre for Policy Alternatives, Briefing Paper, April, Ottawa.

Sinha, S. (2005) 'Neoliberalism and Civil Society: Project and Possibilities', in Saad-Filho and Johnstone, *Neoliberalism: A Critical Reader*, Pluto Press, London.

Skidelsky, R. (1989) *The Social Market Economy*, Social Market Foundation, London.

Smith, T. (2005) 'The Early Experience of NHS Commissioning of Independent Provision and Lessons for the Direction of NHS Reform', *Health Policy Review*, Vol. 1, Issue 1, BMA, London.

Standard and Poor's (2005) *Public Private Partnerships: Global Credit Survey 2005*, May, New York.

Stein, J.G. (2001) 'The Cult of Efficiency', CBC Massey Lectures Series, Anansi Press, Toronto.

Whitfield Dexter (1992) *The Welfare State: Privatisation, Deregulation and Commercialisation of Public Services*, Pluto Press, London.

Whitfield, Dexter. (2001) *Public Services or Corporate Welfare: Rethinking the Nation State in the Global Economy*, Pluto Press, London.

Whitfield, Dexter (2002) 'Impact of Privatisation and Commercialisation on Municipal Services in the UK', *Transfer – Journal of the European Federation of Public Service Unions*, Brussels.

Whitfield, Dexter (2005) 'Labour's Illusory Reforms', *Chartist*, September/October No 216, London.

Whitfield, Dexter (2006) 'Articles of Faith', Education Supplement, *Red Pepper*, No 138, February.

Index

Dexter Whitfield

Dexter Whitfield founded the European Services Strategy Unit (continuing the work of the Centre for Public Services) in 1973, now based in the Sustainable Cities Research Institute, Northumbria University. He has undertaken extensive research and policy analysis of regional/city economies and public sector provision, employment strategies, impact assessment and evaluation, marketisation and privatisation, and modernisation and public management.

He has undertaken commissioned work for a wide range of public sector organisations, local authorities and agencies and worked extensively with trade unions in Britain at branch, regional and national levels, as well as commissioned studies for international trade union federations. He has advised a wide range of community organisations and tenants federations on housing, planning and regeneration policies.

He is the author of *Public Services or Corporate Welfare: The Future of the Nation State in the Global Economy* (2001), *The Welfare State: Privatisation, Deregulation & Commercialisation* (1992) and *Making it Public: Evidence and Action against Privatisation* (1983). He was one of the founding members of *Community Action Magazine* (1973-1995) and *Public Service Action* (1983-1998). He has published many articles in journals and delivered papers and advised public bodies and trade unions in Europe, the United States, Canada, Australia and New Zealand.